BE THE BANK:

CREATING AND INCREASING WEALTH
THROUGH PRIVATE MORTGAGE INVESTING

BY BENJAMIN MICHAEL LYONS

DORRANCE
PUBLISHING CO
EST. 1920
PITTSBURGH, PENNSYLVANIA 15238

Dorrance Publishing Co
585 Alpha Drive
Suite 103
Pittsburgh, PA 15238
Visit our website at *www.dorrancebookstore.com*

ISBN: 978-1-4809-3404-7
eISBN: 978-1-4809-3427-6

Table of Contents

Chapter 1: Introduction and Mission 1
   a. Why write the book
   b. Goals for the reader
   c. Investing 101

Chapter 2: Brief History of Mortgages 11
   a. History of mortgages
   b. What is a mortgage
   c. Mortgage Lender groups
   d. Mortgage Loan Types

Chapter 3: Mortgage Investment Options 29
   a. Why invest in mortgages
   b. The Private mortgage market
   c. Mortgage investment options
   d. Investment returns comparison

Chapter 4: Knowing what to Ask when Investing in Mortgages 47
   a. Primary goal of a mortgage investor
   b. Understanding the key questions to ask
   c. Identify the right mortgage types
   d. Identify and right property types

Chapter 5: Real Mortgage Transactions to get you excited to Invest 73
   a. My story
   b. Transaction that make you scratch your head
   c. Case studies
   d. Mortgage pool
   e. Summary of case studies

Chapter 6: The Basics of Underwriting Mortgage Loans 103
   a. Underwriting overview- My way of thinking
   b. Underwriting the Borrower
   c. Underwriting the Collateral
   d. Payment default predictions

Chapter 7: Comparing Banks vs Private Lenders 117
    a.   Private Lender role
    b.   A banks restrictions to default risk
    c.   Mortgage loan risk classes

Chapter 8: Do it on your Own or Invest in a Mortgage Fund? 125
    a.   Should you become your own Private Lender?
    b.   Should you invest in a loan pool or fund?
    c.   Evaluating the fund

Chapter 9: Getting Started as the Private Lender 139
    a.   Organizing what I need to start Lending
    b.   Pricing the loans
    c.   Marketing for the loans
    d.   Servicing the loans

Chapter 10: Why You Want to "BE THE BANK":
A Look at the Financial Model of Private Lending 149
    a.   Why I love this business
    b.   Successful mortgage lending business model
    c.   The using of debt for Leverage
    d.   BE THE BANK

BE THE BANK:

Chapter 1:
Introduction and Mission

INTRODUCTION

A few years ago, my business partners and I sold a Mortgage Banking Management Company. Part of the negotiated buyout agreement included a non-compete contract. My goals were to invest our newfound capital in an income producing vehicle that would produce passive income in excess of 12% annually.

Having made millions of dollars in the Private Lending, real estate, and Mortgage Banking industries over the years, I knew that I could just re-invest our money in these sectors and earn a very good return on our own invested capital. We decided to stick with our core skills in Mortgage Lending and started a Mortgage and Real Estate Fund. My business partners and I started with three million of our own funds and registered a seventy-five-million-dollar fund so that we could raise additional capital from friends, family and new investors. Prior to starting the fund, our research showed few options for investors that operated Lending Funds and even more surprising was finding that there were very few people who understood the complexities of the mortgage banking and the mortgage investment industry. Furthermore, I found that finding reliable resources within the private mortgage lending sector was extremely difficult and challenging. Where were all the others who were experts in lending money and why was lending money not part of the mainstream investment community, I wondered? It was the research exploration and the present belief that one of the best kept investing secrets is money lending. "Hasn't money lending been around for thousands of years? Is it still a secret or is it a sacred business only available for the banks and the 'others'?" I asked this question to myself and anyone around me I could get to listen. "Who are these 'others' like me? I don't get it", I would shout out, "lending money secured by first mortgages on good real estate at double digit returns is such a good investment. "Where is everyone in this investment sector and why are most investors or the mom and pops not investing in this?" Not even the accredited and the sophisticated investors have any idea about private mortgage lending. It is this revelation that led me to write this book.

My goal for this book is to hopefully educate and inspire you and all investors to explore the wonderful opportunity that exists by investing in the private money lending area. My experiences, opinions and investments along with the ones of several of my business colleagues in mortgages and real estate based assets will provide the foundation for this entire book. Much of this book will be written by me, where I have spent my entire career beginning as a realtor, mortgage broker, Mortgage Banker, Bank Director, Private Lender, Real Estate Investor, Title Company Owner, Construction Company Owner, and Consumer Finance Company Owner, and now Fund Manager. During these past 30 plus years I have owned in excess of 250 investment properties and projects, built a dozen financial services related companies from scratch whereby some of them were sold for good profits and I directly oversaw the mortgage origination and lending in excess of five billion dollars. Approximately two billion dollars-worth of these mortgage loans was in the non-consumer or private sector; specifically, the type we are discussing in this book.

Why the Book?

There are several reasons I chose to write this book but the two main reasons are that I have been very puzzled over my 30-plus year career in lending that the banks have dominated commercial mortgage lending and especially on loans below 5 million. Since lending money was one of the oldest businesses in history, why are the banks almost exclusively the only lenders? The second reason for writing this book is that if more individuals learned about this topic, perhaps this book would provide them the knowledge or theoretical resources to make the leap into the world I have participated for a long time as a private lender.

My conclusion and arguments:

- Banks control the predominant mortgage market for commercial loans
- Banks are regulated by our government and that creates conflicts of use of capital
- Banks inherently need to avoid risk so a percentage of borrowers cannot get the loans
- Banks already use a 10:1 debt-to-capital ratio in their asset allocation to produce a 10% annual return, substantially low for the leverage risk.
- Most people have never thought about "Being the bank"
- Even experienced investors do not consider mortgage lending an investment strategy
- Mortgage Lending is a highly secured investment if performed correctly
- Annual investment returns are substantially higher than many fixed income investments
- When I introduce private lending to others they usually say that it seems too good to be true
- Managing real estate requires more effort than lending money.

My sister inherited some money from a relative of ours about ten years ago and asked me what she should do with her money. I said: "Well, you can give it to an investment advisor who will likely invest it in mutual funds or a diversified portfolio that would suit your investment risk". She said: "Can't I just give to you?" I replied: "Well, yes you can, but you have to trust me and realize that my expertise is lending it out secured by a first mortgage on a property". The good news was that Amy actually worked for me at my mortgage company at the time as a loan processor and auditor so she knew what it meant to secure a property with a mortgage. And so my sister purchased a loan participation for seventy-five thousand dollars and added twenty-five thousand within a short time. Each month she would receive an interest payment for one thousand dollars which was the distribution of the collected mortgage payment from the borrower on the commercial loan where my sister owned the loan participation. This represented a 12% annual return on her 100,000 investment. Over the past many years the original loan that secured my sisters investment has paid off and we reinvested it numerous times to different borrowers all the while my sister has never had an interruption in her monthly payment. One-day last year at my house, during Thanksgiving, my sister and her friend came over and we got into a discussion about her mortgage investment. She said: "Ben, I don't understand why everyone does not invest in mortgages?" She went on to state that every time she has told others about her 12% annual returns and full collateral of her 100,000 she gets back, they replied: "Well, that seems too good to be true and that there must be something illegal or wrong."

About six years ago, when I was managing a Services Contract with a Federally Chartered Bank in Baltimore with the primary objective to grow their Mortgage Lending division, my accounting manager asked me if her brother John, who was a successful business man for forty years, could speak with me. I said: "Sure what for?" She said: "I told him about the mortgage payments you collect over the years that I have worked for you and the rate of returns you were receiving and he asked if he could speak with you to find out what you were doing." So I called and met with John and then John had me meet with his financial advisor and in a third meeting his attorney. The first two meetings ended with John getting told by both his financial advisor and his attorney that lending money was too risky and that even though John was a millionaire, and while John could take his own decision, they advised against investing part of his net worth in mortgages with me. So John called me to tell me the news, and said: "Ben, my financial advisor who has 1.6 million of my retirement and investment accounts, and my attorney, have both advised me to stay away from '*this type of investment*'." Good thing for me that John was stubborn. John asked for a few more meetings and actually hired a different attorney to review what investment strategy we were discussing. I also called his financial advisor and found it very interesting that he knew nothing about mortgage lending and also would not be paid his usual management fee for assets that were NOT under his management. No wonder he would not support such an investment. So, after about 6 meetings and 4 months, John decided to invest 200,000 in a mortgage that was assigned to him. Now, after six or seven years, John has increased his investment substantially and is one of our largest investors in the new fund. I have not calculated exactly, but John has likely received interest distributions that have averaged 13% or more since his initial investment. He has been paid back 100% of his principal on almost all his mortgage investments and continues to tell me: "Ben, given my returns and how good this seems to be going, why is not everyone investing in mortgages?" I give him the same answer as my sister and others: "John, I have absolutely no idea why so many invest in the real estate business but they won't invest in the instrument that is secured by the real estate."

I have many more stories from current and past investors that ask the exact same question. If it's so good, why does not everyone do it and I give the exact same answer each time: "I don't know." My excitement in writing this book is to develop the awareness of mortgage lending as a more "mainstream" investing vehicle. For me, my investing strategy and advice is to always diversify and never put all your eggs in one basket, in the same investment place with the same investment profile. When specifically asked how I invest, I respond that I prefer to have 1/3 of the investments in mutual funds filled with mostly blue chip stocks or related bonds, 1/3 in income-producing real estate, and 1/3 in income-producing mortgages. My argument is that diversification by investment type allows access to multiple industries, geographies, and specific hedges with non-correlated assets such as Mortgages or alternatives.

Goals for you, the reader

My goals for you, the reader, are pretty straightforward:

- **To provide a strong argument that significant opportunities to build and maintain wealth by investing in mortgages exist.**
- **To educate and inform investors on how to successfully invest in Mortgage lending**
- **To inspire qualified investors to invest alongside me in Our Fund**
- **To inspire non-qualified investors to invest in Mortgages on their own.**

You may be asking yourself, at this point: "Who is this guy and why does he think he is the expert on this subject?" Well, for the past 30 years, I have been working in the Mortgage Banking and Real Estate industries. I have personally invested millions of dollars in mortgages and have spent many years originating in excess of 5 billion dollars of mortgages for banks, non-banks, and private lenders. I have been quite successful and have a track record that speaks of this success. My colleagues and I have succeeded in both thriving and distressed environments, over a very long period of time. I have seen competitors come and go, but for the most part, we have continued to prosper through the market shifts and the economic turmoil of the past 30 years. Why? We understand that the key to success in the mortgage lending industry and mortgage investing is based on a set of fundamentals that balance risk management and return on capital. We will discuss more about the "normal" lending rules at banks and non-banks to compare our philosophy with those at other institutions.

What I find most amazing is that the concept of investing in mortgages is not widely publicized. Many savvy investors, even those that invest heavily in real estate, have not or do not understand the value of mortgage investments as an alternative investment. I have traveled the country speaking with Angel Investor groups, Wealth Managers, and Registered Investment Advisors and I often ask two questions at the outset: "By a show of hands how many of you have invested in real estate? "Almost always I see that every hand gets raised. Then I ask the second question: "How many of you have invested in a Mortgage or been a mortgage lender?" Almost no hands get raised to this question. I often leave perplexed asking myself why is it so commonplace that accredited investors are OK investing in real estate but not a mortgage that secures the real estate. I guess it is because many investors fear the unknown, perhaps the stigma with money lenders, or maybe the crash of 2008. I personally have been amazed with this situation, because for me securing an investment by a property at twice my mortgage makes so much sense. I have owned hundreds of income producing properties and given the choice of managing real estate and collecting rent verses collecting a mortgage payment that is secured by the same property I would choose collecting a payment. Certainly real estate ownership can produce good returns under the right circumstances, but the diversity of owning mortgages can also create very good returns with typically less work and often less risk. We will evaluate these points and questions further in this book.

It is my sincere desire, that by the end of this book, you will be inspired and prepared with the information you need to make informed and educated decisions on your investments, specifically if you are considering (or even if you've never considered) mortgage investments.

In each chapter we will begin with a chapter overview listed in bullet points. At the end of each chapter we will have "in other words" summary of the chapter. If you are like me, utilizing the bullet points help with the comprehension of the information and I hope that this approach provides value to the readers.

The advisors and their advice

For the large majority of people their entire lives are spent working towards retirement. Many of them put all or most of their money in an IRA or 401k program hoping that by the time they retire, there will be a nest egg available to carry them through the golden years. They are constantly working to improve their lifestyle, advance their career, start a family or other similar goals, with the future of retirement dangling somewhere ahead. Their retirement investments are typically managed as part of a larger fund and they are offered options based on their risk/reward profile with the end game of producing good returns and a decent nest egg.

The wealth management advice typically comes from wealth managers that have ONLY participated in public equity or debt markets where liquidity is almost certain. Many of these wealth managers have NEVER invested personally or directed a client to invest in anything non-public, non-liquid, or considered an alternative investment. Why is this so, and does this answer the question asked earlier in this book about why very few investors have ever considered investing in mortgages? It is because none of the advisors have ever considered this to be a safe or a good solution for a portion of one's investment portfolio. The reasons for me suggest that these wealth managers typically do not have the knowledge or authority personally or through their companies to support and recommend such investments.

During this same time frame, the entrepreneurial types are often busy building, buying and selling companies. They may become angel investors where historically, they may experience 3-4 business failures and an additional 4-5 exits which will return only a modest return on investment. Typically, just one or two investments out of ten provide most of the portfolio return, with a 10-30x ROI expected on these few successes. With a small fraction of investments providing the bulk of the reward, angels should consider a significant number of diversified investments to optimize ROI.

It's ironic that we spend 30-50 years working towards retirement but only spend a fraction of that time thinking about how we will preserve the money we have saved, to ensure that it lasts. As a matter of fact, most of us don't think about this issue until we are near or already retired. But, once you have the nest egg, you want to protect it and make sure it's working as hard as it can be. Once you start to live off that nest egg, you want to ensure that your capital is still growing, but that it is also properly preserved and protected. The biggest nest egg in the world could be meaningless if you don't have a plan for the preservation of the capital.

GO WITH WHAT YOU KNOW

Most investors tend to invest in things they know or are familiar with. Often, wherever an investor accumulates much of their wealth, he or she tends to be 'go-to' in terms of future investments. Those who made their wealth in the tech industry tend to invest in technology. Those who spent their career in health care industries may be drawn to life sciences. Certainly, within these industries, there are thousands of specialties, niches, options and diversification strategies. Within each niche, there are pros and cons, inherent risks and rewards. Each investor must explore, or pay someone to explore, these strategies.

"I've got a guy." Almost everyone has a guy. You know the guy. He's a brilliant investor. He's made my friend millions. He's got a proven method. Whatever the story, all of us either "know a guy" or know somebody who's "got a guy." That's good. But, regardless of who you know, you need to know what you don't know. You don't just invest in things because somebody says it's a good investment. Make sure that you're somewhat educated on the types of investments you, your advisor or "your guy" are making. You don't have to be an expert, but you shouldn't expect that "your guy" is going to make every decision right. Two heads are better than one – shouldn't yours be one of them?

One must keep in mind an important quote from the world's most famous investor, Warren Buffet. He said "Never test the depth of the river with both

---

[1] Source: "Asset Allocation and Portfolio Strategy for Angel Investors" by William H. Payne, Kauffman Foundation.

feet." There are important lessons here. One must be educated. Stay in tune with your investment strategies and the types of investments you are making. The Internet can educate you in a short period of time on a wealth of topics. If you are adding a new category, industry, company or opportunity to your portfolio, be sure you know something about it. Most importantly, if you are not a professional investor, do your research on who you are trusting with your money and ask key questions before you invest. Later in this book, I will address the key questions you need to ask when investing in mortgages or mortgage funds.

ADVANTAGES TO ALTERNATIVES

The stock market may be riding high today or at the time you are reading this book, however at the time of this writing the Dow Jones has produced a less than a 2% increase this year through beginning of October 2015 and over the past ten years has provided an average return of 5.61%. Countless stories exist about investors who put all their eggs in this one strategy and lose their entire fortune. For this reason, many advisors recommend not only diversification, but including alternatives as portion of your overall investment strategy. Why?

Alternative assets can bring significant benefits to investment portfolios through diversifying exposure away from traditional fixed income and equity assets. Alternative assets are no longer the exclusive to the super-wealthy; in fact, the average retail investor can have access to a wide range of alternative asset strategies through traditional vehicles, including mutual funds, exchange-traded funds (ETFs) and exchange-traded notes (ETNs).

There are many varieties of alternative assets, but a common feature and key benefit is a low level of correlation with fixed-income and equity markets, and therefore a measurable degree of independence from systematic market risk factors. Alternative assets can further be categorized into non-directional or hedge strategies, which profit from the construction of offsetting positions in equity, fixed income or other instruments, and directional positions in asset classes such as commodities, global equities and real estate.

Alternative assets are accessible via traditional retail products, such as mutual funds and hedge funds, and other vehicles targeted to sophisticated high net worth investors. Combining different types of alternative assets into a portfolio can produce a more optimal asset allocation, and performance benefits that are particularly visible during sustained periods of weak equity market performance.

In Other Words

- ❖ I was driven to explain mortgage lending and wrote this book.
- ❖ The book is to provide a strong argument that significant opportunities to build and maintain wealth by investing in mortgages exist.
- ❖ The book is to educate and inform investors on how to successfully invest in Mortgage lending.
- ❖ The book is to inspire qualified investors to invest alongside me in Our Fund.
- ❖ The book is to inspire non-qualified investors to invest in Mortgages on their own.

I hope you enjoy the book and benefit greatly from the information provided!

BE THE BANK:

Chapter 2:
Brief History of Mortgages

HERE'S WHAT WE COVER IN THIS CHAPTER

- Review brief history of mortgage lending
- Review of the mortgage lenders of today by groups
- Review the various mortgage types or options
- Review the 2008 financial meltdown & how it related to mortgages
- Review financial events that I had to navigate and their impact
- Chapter Summary

Now let's take a look at the history of lending and more specifically mortgage lending. All private mortgage investors should have a basic knowledge of the mortgage business in order to do their jobs properly.

HISTORY OF MORTGAGE LENDING

The history of providing mortgages has its roots in ancient civilization. Many scholars hypothesize that debtors swore a pledge to obtain property before the advent of the mortgage. During these times, the "mortgagor" would make an agreement with a "mortgagee" to exchange property for repayment over time.[2] The mortgage is a widely used form of money lending because, in most cases, the property remains with the debtor in the good faith that the debt will be

---

[2]http://www.randomhistory.com/1-50/037mortgage.html.

paid—with interest, of course. In other words, *the mortgage is meant to be a beneficial arrangement for both parties.*

Commercial banks, and later mutual savings banks and property banks, greatly expanded into the early nineteenth century beginning in the port cities and working inward, adapting to the unique characteristics and needs of each new region. The National Bank Act of 1864 established charters for national banks and greater security and oversight for the federal treasury to develop a nationalized currency (primarily to finance the Civil War), replacing the individual state and bank bonds.

By the early 1900s, mortgages "featured variable interest rates, high down payments, and short maturities." And before the Great Depression, homeowners typically renegotiated their loans every year. Mortgages began to take more modern shape as a result of the intervention of the federal government during the Great Depression. The most important institutions that resulted were the Home Owner's Loan Corporation (1933), the Federal Housing Administration (1936), and the Federal National Mortgage Association (1938) later known as Fannie Mae or FNMA. The Depression-era institutions were designed to provide government-sponsored bonds to reinstate mortgages in default by extending terms and fixing rates to create self-amortizing loans for the borrower. Other provisions were for mortgage insurance and investing confidence, especially to stabilize mortgages in less-affluent communities. The Government National Mortgage Association or GNMA (Ginnie Mae) was established in 1968 to "bring uniformity to the mortgage market and create financial instruments that would help keep the mortgage market liquid from the mid-1980s until today." In 1970, the Federal Home Loan Mortgage Corporation or FHLMC, known as Freddie Mac, was formed to further promote home ownership by "providing liquidity in the [secondary] mortgage marketplace."[3] By 2003, governmental mortgage institutions held 43 percent of the total mortgage market. Beginning in the late 1990's, liquidity for mortgages began to grow from Wall Street firms who developed many variations of mortgage backed securities that were pools of loans with terms like "alternative 'A', Option Arms, Stated Income, High LTV, and Subprime". The landscape of the mortgage market shifted from the early 1990's until 2008 from one that was

[3]Green, Richard K. and Susan M. Wachter. "The American Mortgage in Historical and International Context." The Journal of Economic Perspectives, Vol. 19, No. 4. (Autumn, 2005), pp. 93-114

predominantly a depository bank originated industry to a non-depository origination industry. In other words, the secondary market for mortgages went from traditional bankers to Wall Street bankers. Since the crash of 2008, the origination and ownership of mortgages has shifted back to either a depository originated mortgage or a non-depository "agency eligible" mortgage market, meaning only government underwritten or eligible loans.

MODERN DAY MORTGAGE

In basic terms, a mortgage is a loan that is secured by a lien on real estate. In some states a third party is added to the mortgage document and this changes the document name to a deed of trust. For the purposes of this book, we will consider a deed of trust or mortgage, are synonymous given that both legal agreements between the borrower and the lender create a security on the real estate in the event of default. Throughout this book we may be speaking about a mortgage or a deed of trust and intend to use these words interchangeably. It is typical that accompanying the mortgage or a deed of trust is a referring or inter-connected note. If there is a related mortgage or deed of trust note, the note spells out in more detail the terms and conditions of the loan where the mortgage or deed of trust is the security instrument that provides the collateral against the real estate. The note is also referred to as the borrowers promise to pay. We will be discussing the loan package to include the loan closing documents in further chapters in this book.

WHO ARE THE MORTGAGE LENDERS TODAY?

I am told often that when I speak with people about the lending and banking industry I tend to make things complicated because I get into too much detail. So unless you are in the mortgage lending industry you might find some of what I am discussing complicated to understand. I apologize for this level of detail but it might prove useful to the complete understanding of the entire mortgage lending industry and how one can compare the typical mortgage bank to a private lender. Remember that my goal for this book is to justify and explain why being a private mortgage lender or investing in mortgages makes sense. But to understand my point of view and argued reasoning I should explain in detail the mortgage lending and mortgage banking industry.

In the most recent era, in the mortgage lending or mortgage banking industry we can organize the lending entities, institutions or structures for providing mortgages to consumers (primary homeowner occupied real estate loans) and investors (commercial and income producing real estate loans) into groups or categories. It is important for the reader of this book to understand the difference between a *consumer mortgage loan* and a *commercial mortgage loan*. We will cover and expand this distinction in more detail later in several chapters of this book. The main focus of this book is on commercial mortgages. These should be the instruments used by all investors who want to make money as a private lender or mortgage investor. In this book there is much discussion about consumer mortgages and how they are originated, the types and the marketplace for investors, however, we are only providing this information as a reference and to properly explain the entire mortgage lending and mortgage investment options.

Before we provide the various groups of lenders that provide mortgages today I want to separate the mortgage industry into several categories. The first is the Mortgage Originator or "Primary Market". The "Primary Market" interacts directly with the consumer or borrower. This could be a mortgage broker taking the information and passing it on to a mortgage banker to fund the loan or it could be the mortgage banker. A mortgage broker arranges loans for a fee and passes the info on to a mortgage banker to fund the loan. Prior to the 2008 financial crisis, 70% of all mortgage originations (Primary Market) began with mortgage brokers. This figure has fallen substantially since the financial meltdown. After the crisis ended, the marketplace had less than half the number of mortgage brokers when compared to the period before 2008. The primary market once dominated by mortgage brokers is now made up by originators such as banks, Credit Unions, Wall Street Investors, Private and Public Mortgage Bankers, Finance companies, and individuals. The secondary market buys the loans from the primary market originators. After 2008, the Government-owned or -controlled agencies make up 90% of the secondary market in consumer mortgage lending. See the chart below where this is illustrated.

The information in this section identifies mortgages to the consumers and commercial mortgages to investors but more importantly breaks down the info by groups.

- <u>Group 1</u>: *A local, National, or Savings bank originated the mortgage loan where the loan would be held for investment by the bank. (Held for investment strategy)* This means the bank originates the loan based on their own internal set of guidelines and the bank keeps the loan on its books and is responsible for the borrower payment performance, servicing and default risk. In this example the loan could be a consumer loan or an investor (commercial) loan.

  Example: Wells Fargo, Bank of America, Chase, smaller banks.

- <u>Group 2</u>: *A local, National, or Savings bank has originated the loan under one of the guidelines of the GSE (Government-sponsored enterprises) or secondary market investor with the sole intention to sell the loan once funded. (Held for sale strategy)* These GSE are Fannie Mae, Freddie Mac, and Ginnie Mae. They typically purchase consumer mortgage loans, whereas on the secondary market, investment or commercial mortgage loans are sold and converted into CMBS (Commercial Mortgage Backed Securities). In the held for sale strategy, the bank originally utilized its own money but intended to sell the loan to one of the GSE or secondary market investors even before the loan was originated. The GSE or the secondary market investors will agree to purchase the loan if the bank properly underwrote the loan in accordance with the mandated guidelines. The bank in this case was a conduit or pass through entity for the purpose of generating a service to a borrower and to generate fee income. This type of strategy poses very little balance sheet or interest rate risk to the originating bank because the loan was only held on the banks books for a short period of time. Should the mortgage be a commercial loan, then it would likely be sold off to an intermediary then turned into a Commercial Mortgage Backed Security. The bank often would retain the servicing rights of the loan; however the ownership of the asset was sold to another investor. The servicing bank in this case would not likely have any interest rate or capital risk.

  Example: Wells Fargo, Bank of America, Chase, Smaller banks

- <u>Group 3</u>: *A local, Regional or National non-bank originated the mortgage loan, where the loan would be held for investment by the non-bank. (Held for investment strategy)* This follows the same reasoning as Group 1 but with a non-bank. This means the non-bank originates the loan based on their own internal set of guidelines and the non-bank keeps the loan on its books and is responsible for the borrower payment performance, servicing and default risk. Today, there are very few of these non-banks and the reason for this is that in order for the non-bank to be able to fund a large volume of loans they would have to have a huge amount of capital and balance sheet. Unlike a bank, this type of lender would have to rely on capital or debt sources to finance the company from something other than the deposits a depository bank can generate. Our banking system allows the bank to take in 8-12 times its capital in deposits and that typically allows it to grow its balance sheet in a larger extent than a non-depository bank. It would be very difficult for a non-depository bank to leverage its capital 10:1, especially after the 2008 financial crisis. In much of my career running a mortgage banking firm that was considered a non-depository bank, the highest debt-to-equity ratio I could obtain was 5:1. This means that unlike the government's allowance of a depositor bank to borrow up to 12 times its capital, I was only able to borrow 5 times the capital as a non-depository bank. This is a key distinction and discussion in future sections of this book.

Example: Any non-bank or consumer finance company that originates and holds the mortgages. Very few of these exist. Some are private equity and hedge funds, some are insurance companies.

- Group 4: *A local or National non-depository Bank originated the mortgage loan where the loan would be held for sale by the non-depository bank. (Held for sale strategy)* The reasoning is the same as for Group 2 above but for non-depository banks. In this example, the non-depository bank originally utilized its own money but intended to sell the loan to one of the GSE or secondary market investors even before the loan was originated. The GSE or secondary market investor will agree to purchase the loan if the non-depository bank properly underwrote the loan in accordance with the mandated guidelines. The non-depository bank in this case was a conduit or pass through entity for the purpose of generating a service to a borrower and to generate fee income. This means the non-depository bank originates the loan based on standard secondary market guidelines as established by the secondary market.

This type of strategy poses very little balance sheet or interest rate risk to the originating non-depository bank because the mortgage loan is not held on the non-depository bank's books very long. Should the mortgage be a commercial mortgage, the loan would likely be sold off to an intermediary then turned into a Commercial Mortgage Backed Security. Prior to the 2008 financial collapse, this group of non-depository mortgage bankers represented a very large segment of the "primary" mortgage market. After 2008 this group has shrank to a fraction of what it was before 2008, pushing many primary market mortgage loan originators into depository banks or out of business.

Example: Quicken Loans is the biggest player in this category for residential mortgages. Insurance companies, private equity and hedge funds focus on investment or commercial mortgages.

Primary Mortgage Originators	Group #	Secondary market buyers from originators (residential)	Secondary market buyers from originators (commercial)
Mortgage Brokers	Not originating group because brokers do not fund loans, just present them to banks or bankers for a fee.	Does not sell to secondary	Does not sell to secondary
Mortgage Bankers	Groups # 3 & 4	Ginnie Mae, Fannie Mae, Freddie Mac, Banks, Wall Street (pre-2008)	Wall Street, insurance companies, banks
Banks	Groups #1 & 2	Ginnie Mae, Fannie Mae, Freddie Mac, Banks, Wall Street (pre-2008)	Wall Street, insurance companies, other banks
Credit Unions	Groups #1 & 2	Ginnie Mae, Fannie Mae, Freddie Mac, Banks, Wall Street (pre-2008)	Wall Street, insurance companies, banks
Finance Companies	Group # 3 & 4	Typically does not sell to secondary for consumer loans	Wall Street, insurance companies, banks
Private Lenders	Group # 3	Typically does not sell to secondary for consumer loans	Typically does not sell the loans. Could sell to Wall Street, insurance companies

MORTGAGE OPTIONS OR TYPES

We explained in the previous section the various Groups that originate mortgages but that does not really make it easy to understand what "Types" of mortgages these groups produce. There are a large number of mortgage types or loan structures to consider as a borrower and as an investor. The types are broken down by their overall characteristic, such as who the primary or secondary originating group is. This list happens to be my list and may vary from bank to bank, non-bank to non-bank and is not intended to include every mortgage type that was ever developed. This list is meant to give the reader an overview or basic understanding of the generic mortgage structures.

Mortgage Types

o   *First Mortgages* – The mortgage lender is in a recorded first lien position only. In other words, the mortgage lender has a recorded first lien in the public records in the county where the property is located and evidenced by a deed of trust or mortgage. In the event of a default and foreclosure, the lender in first lien position would get paid first from the proceeds of sale.

o   *Second Mortgages* - The mortgage lender is in a recorded second mortgage lien position only. This means the lender is in a recorded second mortgage position behind a first mortgage, so that if a foreclosure took place and the property was sold, the first mortgage lender gets paid first and then the second lien holder gets paid if there is sufficient money after payment to the first lender. As an obvious rule, this makes investing in a second mortgage much riskier than a first mortgage.

o   *Credit Lines* - A credit line or line of credit is called an "open end mortgage" and acts like a credit card, where funds can be taken out and paid back repeatedly throughout the term of the loan. This type of mortgage can be a first or a second mortgage lien. Many banks and non-banks provide credit lines in second lien positions often referred to as "Home Equity Lines of Credit or HELOC". The benefit to both borrower and lender with a HELOC is that the loan allows a borrower to draw up and down on the cash available from the line without having to re-close or re-sign each time.

o *Closed End Mortgages* – A closed end mortgage loan has a specific re-payment period and no ability to draw down on funds once paid back. This loan can be a first or a second mortgage. The majority of the "standard" consumer mortgages are originated as closed end mortgages. The most common closed end mortgage is the 30-year fixed rate closed end mortgage.

o *Fixed Rate vs. Variable Rate mortgage loans* – A fixed rate mortgage loan has an interest rate that does not fluctuate, whereas a variable rate mortgage loan can change based on a defined index and margin such as the Wall Street Journal Prime Rate plus 2%. The benefits to the borrower of an adjustable versus a fixed rate loan are that the initial interest rates can be lower compared to a fix rate should the overall interest rate on the market decrease. The fixed rate could also not be beneficial to a lender, if the overall interest rate on the market would register a rally. Adjustable rate loans can benefit the lender or investor, because when interest rates rise, so does the rate of return to the lender or investor. This eliminates the interest rate risk that a fixed rate loan could create. Many investor or commercial loans are originated as variable rate loans so the bank or non-bank does not have long term interest rate risk. Most consumer mortgages are structured as fixed rates.

o *Interest only mortgage loans* – An interest only mortgage loan requires the borrower to make monthly interest payments, but not require the borrower to pay any money towards the principal loan amount. In this scenario, the principal loan amount is not typically impacted, meaning the borrower will be responsible for the principal balance at payoff or at a set time as defined in the mortgage or mortgage note. This loan is ideal for a borrower that may be paying off the loan in a short-time period or may be reselling the property or refinancing the property in the short term. This loan typically has the lowest monthly payments as a result of the borrower ONLY paying the interest to the lender.

o *Amortizing mortgage loans* - An amortizing mortgage loan requires the borrower to make principal and interest payments based on a decreasing loan balance until repaid. This type of mortgage loan is most common among consumer mortgage borrowers and lenders. Many individuals blame the 2008 financial collapse on lenders not requiring borrowers to contract amortizing loans, whereby requiring the borrower to lower the balance of the mortgage each month. Many secondary market investors believe that the amortizing mortgage loan carries less risk than an interest only loan because the outstanding loan balance is decreasing every time a payment is made.

o *Balloon payment provision* – This loan type requires the balance of the loan to be due at a point in time whereby the entire principal balance is due and payable. For example, a 30 year amortization with a 5 year balloon payment due. This can be good for the borrower if the balloon feature reduces the interest rate during the period prior to the balloon payment but could also be very risky to the borrower if the borrower cannot refinance or repay the balance of the mortgage when the balloon payment is due. Many depository banks offer balloon mortgages to their commercial mortgage borrowers to protect the bank against long term interest rate increases. Balloon payment loans mainly benefit the lender or investor.

o *Commercial mortgage loans* - This type of mortgage loan is for business purposes only. It is not considered a consumer mortgage loan and cannot be secured by a person's primary residence unless the borrower and lender both document that 100% of the loan is used for business purposes. A rental or investment property is an example of a commercial loan. It is very important for any investor that is considering investing in mortgages to understand the distinction between a consumer and commercial mortgage loan. We often speak about a commercial or investor loan as a loan for commercial purposes only however, it is an important point to explain to our readers in this book that the underlying real estate can be residentially zoned. It gets somewhat confusing that a commercial loan is made on a residential property but the key is that the money that is loaned to the borrower is for investment or commercial purposes only. Throughout this book

I will be giving advice to our readers and investors to ONLY invest in commercial loans. I will explain more on this reasoning in other chapters.

o   *Residential or consumer mortgage loans* - This type of loan is typically secured by an individual's primary residence or a second home. A rental property is not typically considered a consumer loan. As discussed in the section on commercial mortgage loans, in this book I will explain and educate the readers the difference between a consumer and commercial mortgage loan however we will NOT be focusing on the consumer mortgage loan, as this is not the type of mortgage an investor should be looking to directly invest in, however there are many good investments that can be made in consumer mortgages. We will address investing in consumer mortgage later in this book.

o   *Construction or renovation mortgage loans* – This type of mortgage is used for the purposes of building, renovating or improving any type of real estate. These mortgage loans typically have a construction reserve established at closing (to cover costs of renovation up to the approved value of the loan). The loan interest is typically billed monthly based on the principal mortgage balance advanced by the lender. This type of mortgage loan typically is considered short-term and has a usual length of 4 - 24 months, depending on the construction or renovation project. Not all lenders provide construction or renovation loans, because it requires the lender to have an expertise in managing the construction or rehabilitation projects of the borrower or contractor. For this reason, these loans can be priced higher than the "standard" mortgage market as a result of the inherent risk and cost of construction management in addition to the borrower payment management. If a lender can effectively manage this business it can often generate higher loan fees and increased loan yields. The LYNK mortgage capital fund that is managed by me and my associates focuses on these type of mortgage loans specifically to maximize the return of the fund.

o   *Bridge mortgage loans* – This type of mortgage loan allows a borrower to borrow on a certain property with the purpose of buying another for the time period until the original property is sold. So for example you own a rental property valued at $200,000 and it is free of any mortgage loans and you want to buy another rental property for $200,000 but you do not want to utilize any of your cash to buy the new property. In this example the mortgage lender would secure both properties and advance 100% of the purchase price plus closing costs so that an investor can buy the home without any new cash. This is a great way for borrower and lender to take advantage of the equity that is in the free and clear investment property. In this scenario a lender can secure one or both of the properties at the time of closing until the old property gets sold.

o   *Blanket loans* – This type of loan is used to secure more than one property as collateral. One mortgage loan secures multiple properties. This is often used similar to a bridge loan where one mortgage is utilized so that the borrower can utilize the equity in one or more properties without having to secure several different loans. In our discussion about leverage or the use of debt to grow the portfolio and rate of return we will be utilizing a blanket loan to achieve this result.

THE FINANCIAL COLLAPSE OF 2008
AS BLAMED ON THE MORTGAGE AND BANKING INDUSTRY

Since 2008 I have been asked many times about whom or what was to blame and what contributed to the financial meltdown of 2007 through 2009. Some blame the government for pushing lenders to expand home ownership. Many blame Wall Street bankers for peddling questionable sub-prime loans packaged in pools or securities. Some blame Fannie Mae and Freddie Mac for lowering their credit and underwriting standards. I have heard it all from the greedy investment bankers, loan officers, mortgage lenders, and really everyone seems to have an opinion of who was to blame. Well, since you asked me (ok, perhaps you didn't ask) I will offer my own opinion of the relationship or correlation between mortgage lending and the financial collapse leading up to 2008. Please keep in mind these are my opinions. The premise of the collapse was that trillions of dollars were invested by the public, investment banks, large and small banks, countries, governments, and almost everyone seemed to have some type of investment directly or indirectly in mortgage instruments. These mortgage instruments were packaged into securities and the securities were sold off as Mortgage Backed or Collateralized Debt obligations. All of these obligations, regardless of the structure, relied on the majority of borrowers to make monthly payments and that the underlying real estate would protect the capital or debt obligation in the event the borrower did not perform on the payments. I will do my best from my standpoint to argue the reasons for the rise and fall of these events and not go too far into the weeds of detail so that it makes sense to all the readers.

- We can start with the 1980's and review the data on the Ginnie Mae (Federal Housing Administration/ Veterans Affairs), Fannie Mae and Freddie Mac (Conventional loans) historical loan performances that were good, with relatively low delinquency and defaults of about 2%. The mortgage backed securities market of these mortgages, including the Wall Street folks, were likely feeling positive about their credit guidelines, data and algorithms that allowed them to properly predict and manage default risks given the 20 years of data leading up to the year 1992.

- In 1992, the Housing and Community Development Act of 1992 was approved in congress. The Act amended the charter of Fannie Mae and Freddie Mac to reflect the Democratic Congress' view that the GSEs "... have an affirmative obligation to facilitate the financing of affordable housing for low- and moderate-income families in a manner consistent with their overall public purposes, while maintaining a strong financial condition and a reasonable economic return." For the first time, the GSEs were required to meet "affordable housing goals" set annually by the Department of Housing and Urban Development (HUD) and approved by Congress.

- In the late 1990's and into the early 2000's my belief was that the Wall Street investment bankers were reviewing the stated income loan tranches from Fannie Mae (FNMA) mortgage backed securities and concluded that a higher Loan To Value and No Income model could be managed provided the risk was priced into the loan. I was part of this primary origination market at the time and remember the list of

Wall Street investors calling me for loan product and each month I saw the guidelines getting more aggressive and expanded to feed the appetite of the mortgage securitizations or loan pools. Even though I thought it made no sense to me, I was offered very high premiums to sell the Wall Street firms loan pools. Let's revisit the concept of "stated income" briefly here and I will go into great detail in later chapters in this book on underwriting. FNMA had for years offered stated income loan products but this product was ONLY for self-employed people and only if they had a very large down payment, excellent credit, and substantial reserves to make payments. The era of fundamentally sound stated income loans changed to one that increased the loan to values from 70% to 100%. Additionally, the substantially reduced cash requirements for the borrowers and the substantially lowered credit standards, regardless of the increased interest rate on the loan, turned out to be disastrous and caused defaults to skyrocket. This new underwriting also artificially increased home ownership to the wrong borrowers for a temporary time period and because buyers could obtain credit, this caused an artificially induced buyer demand driving real estate values higher. This was almost like a Ponzi scheme because as long as the borrower could keep flipping the house to pay off the loan it gave the illusion that the borrower could afford the repayment of the loan. The reason the FNMA stated income loans had performed in the 1980's and 1990's is that the borrowers had a large cash down payment and documented reserves whereas the "new era" of stated income loans required neither large cash from borrower or sufficient reserves.

- By 2005 FHA originations had fallen dramatically in exchange for the stated income and high loan to value loans. FNMA contributed to the mess by introducing the Option Adjustable-Rate Mortgage (ARM) program, whereby the initial rate or lower payment was all a borrower needed to do to qualify taking no consideration that once the interest rate adjusted the borrower had no documented ability to afford the higher payment. While this did open up many new buyers that would not otherwise qualify for mortgage financing it only temporarily created the exact same issue as the stated income loan.

- The result of the stated income, high loan to value loans, Option ARM loans drove home ownership to an all-time high and pushed real estate values up as much as 50%. Similar to the dot-com bust of 1999-2001, the underlying fundamentals were removed from the equation. Borrower affordability was NO longer the most important driver in the decision to approve a loan. The good news is that after the 2008 financial collapse, the fundamentals of lending have returned.

- I am writing this book at the end of 2015 and my last thought on the financial collapse of 2008 is that like most investments there is a way to properly risk-adjust mortgages but it requires the connectivity of the primary and secondary market makers to join in the risk throughout the life of the loan. The person that originates the loan needs to be responsible for the performance risk and not solely the origination.

2008 financial collapse conclusion
o   Historical data on loan performance suggested mortgage borrowers will likely always pay
o   Congress pushed for more home ownership and the lenders lowered standards
o   Wall Street loan default models for stated income loans were wrong
o   Wall Street loan default models for high loan to values and lower credit scores were wrong
o   FNMA loan model for Option ARM was flawed
o   The number of buyers into real estate market was artificially increased
o   Supplies were artificially driven down and prices were increased
o   A short-term sense of wealth was artificially created, because of underwriting changes that proved to be incorrect.
o   Once defaults started, the real estate values plummeted and losses began

Not many would argue that the mortgage industry along with the US financial markets have seen their fair share of ups and downs over the years. The mortgage industry has been very cyclical indeed since my career began. The very concept of a mortgage, as stated earlier, is to provide a **beneficial arrangement for both the borrower and the lender**. So, if that is the premise, why is the industry subject to such highs and lows? Of course, there are factors, but I would argue that this scenario occurs most often when the industry fails to follow certain principles of common sense. My approach to lending and what all lenders need to do to keep from getting crushed as the down cycle begins is:

- Only loan to those companies or individuals who show a documented desire and ability to repay the payments and the loan,
- Have the argued financial wherewithal to support themselves and their debts throughout the term of the loan,
- Make sure the borrower has something meaningful to gain and something meaningful to lose if they default on the loan,
- Do not lend more than a certain percentage of what the property is currently worth,
- Do not lend more than the property may be worth if borrower fails to fulfill their obligation (make payments on their loan), and
- Do not lend more than the property may be worth if the lender has to take over the loan, fix up and/or resell the property.

Let's go back to talking about me again (my favorite subject)

In my career which began a few years before the savings and loan crisis, there have been a handful of market corrections and economic challenges that faced the US economy and allowed me to learn some valuable lessons. I have often said that the economic events that caused me to lose money were important lessons for me and that I should know more than most about how to manage the risk of recurring market changes and contractions. Since my mortgage lending and real estate career began in 1984, I illustrate below some of the world and US economic events or scenarios that affected the lending conditions.

- The savings and loan crisis of 1985-88 *(I got a good education at such a young age)*
- The recession of the early 1990's *(I learned about recession for the first time)*
- The rapid increase of interest rates by the Federal Reserve in 1994 *(I learned about business drying up rapidly & real estate values changing as a result)*

- The Asian financial crisis of 1997 *(did not pay that much attention because my mortgage lending company was making great profits)*
- The Russian financial crisis of 1998 *(I lost a lot of money as a result of mortgage pools being de-valued due to this world event and it cost me about 5 million dollars)*
- The dot com bubble and bust from 1999 to 2001*(It was strange in this period that companies were valued at billions of dollars but never earned a penny. I did not get it)*
- The 9/11 terrorist attack causing havoc in the financial markets *(A terrible day in America)*
- Finally, the granddaddy of my and likely everyone's career, the financial meltdown of 2008 *(I have an entire chapter on this subject)*

In Other Words

- ❖ Mortgage Lending has been around since ancient times
- ❖ The mortgage lending in the 1900's went through many changes beginning with the great depression of 1929 when FHA was introduced
- ❖ The Government-sponsored agencies played a predominant role in creating liquidity for the mortgage market
- ❖ Mortgages are funded by banks and non-banks
- ❖ Banks and non-banks originate mortgages that are held for investment or kept on their books
- ❖ Many banks and non-banks immediately sell loans to secondary market investors
- ❖ There are many different types of mortgages to consider
- ❖ Mortgages to consumers, unlike the ones to investors, are sold to different secondary markets
- ❖ The 2008 financial meltdown can be partially blamed on reduced lending standards
- ❖ The author of this book has been through many market challenges that have provided great experiences and lessons on how to protect invested capital.
- ❖ The performance of mortgage investments has a lot to do with lender experience and lending strategies.

BE THE BANK:

Chapter 3:
Mortgage Investment Options

HERE'S WHAT WE COVER IN THIS CHAPTER

- **Why should you invest in mortgages?**
- **Review what mortgage investments are available to investors.**
- **Review Mortgage-Backed Securities and their risks and benefits**
- **Review a historical comparison of Equities, Treasuries, Real Estate investments**
- **Chapter Summary**

WHY INVEST IN MORTGAGES?

In this chapter I will discuss in more depth why to invest in mortgages. Many people have made, and lost, a great deal of money from owning and managing of real estate. Certainly, there are inherent risks with any investment. But, the one unique proposition that real estate investments typically offer over other types of investments is that the investment in real estate is secured or tied to some type of physical asset is tangible and it will likely always be there (unless it burns down). This is different than investing in a start-up, an invention, or a new technology – perhaps all great investments, but often with no tangible collateral or with no guarantees on return of capital if something goes wrong and you need to liquidate. What attracted me to the real estate and mortgage side of investing was the added sense of security because there is a physical asset securing your capital known as a deed, in the case of owning real estate, or deed of trust, in the case of mortgage.

Mortgages, you say? "Why would anyone want to invest in mortgages? That's way too risky! I don't know how to lend money! How do I know what I'm investing in?" If you are new to investing, these may be the thoughts running through your head. This is another big reason I have written this book. Perhaps one of the biggest challenges with investing in mortgages is public perception and/or misperception. As mentioned earlier, my colleagues and I found a lack of educational resources to provide industry insight, objective perspective and general guidance on mortgage investment strategies. In addition, even if we can show you why investing in mortgages makes sense, there are very few resources that can direct you to these investment opportunities or teach you the basics on how to become your own bank or "Be the Bank" as a private lender. Finally, if you decide to invest in mortgage pools or a mortgage fund, how do you vet the groups or individuals that you will partner with, on these opportunities?

The purpose of this book will be to inspire you to invest and educate you on mortgage lending strategies, real estate values, borrower credit and other crucial elements that impact mortgage lending decisions. I hope that the information I share will educate you to the extent that you will understand the value that mortgage investments can add to your investment portfolio and the best ways in which to evaluate them, so that your experience as a passive mortgage investor or as an active one is positive.

WHAT MORTGAGE INVESTMENTS
EXIST IN THE MARKETPLACE?

One of the reasons I have chosen to write this book is to argue that mortgage investing should be as mainstream as real estate investing. We discuss throughout this book my philosophy on investing a portion of your portfolio in alternative investments and more specifically investments that are not correlated to the broader markets such as stocks and bonds. Let's review in this section where an investor could invest in the mortgage market and the differences in these investments within the mortgage investment arena. What you will find is that there are very few real good options today to invest in mortgages of any kind. You could own a bank that makes mortgage loans but then you really own equity in the bank and not just the mortgages at the bank. Let's examine the table below to view the options today's investors have, either directly or indirectly, in owning a mortgage related investment.

Today's mortgage investment options

Mortgage Investment Options	Investor requirement	Risk of loss	Financial benefit	Liquidity
Buy Residential Mortgage Backed Security	Purchase from Broker, non-accredited can invest	Low risk	Slightly higher than treasuries	Yes
Buy Commercial Mortgage Backed Securities	Purchase fro m Broker, non – accredited can invest	Low risk	Slightly higher than treasuries	Yes
Buy Collateral-ized Mortgage Obligation	Purchase from Broker, non-accredited can invest	Low, moderate and high risk	Varies but higher than treasuries	Typically yes, depends on specific Bond purchased
Invest in a mort-gage Pool or Fund	Purchase from broker or directly, typically only ac-credited investors can invest	Moderate to high risk*	Substantially higher than treasuries	Typically Not Liquid
Become your own Private Lender	Obtain the knowledge to in-vest directly. Non accredited can invest	Moderate to high risk*	Substantially higher than treasuries	Typically Not Liquid

**Risk is based on many factors depending on the investment and associated loans securing the investment. As a private lender and mortgage fund manager I often explain that the investment risk is low to moderate, however, the broader investment community would view it as high.

Let's dig deeper into each one of the investment options and get educated on what makes the most sense to you, the investor, should you consider investing in mortgages.

Investment Option #1 -Purchase Residential Mortgage-Backed Securities
Residential mortgage-backed securities are fixed-income investments that generate interest revenue through pools of mortgages. Sometimes they are referred

to as MBS or "pools" or "mortgage pass-through certificates." MBS investors own an interest in a pool of mortgages that serve as the underlying asset for the MBS. When homeowners make their monthly payment that money is passed through to the MBS investors or "certificate holders." Most mortgage-backed securities that are backed by residential real estate are issued by three primary agencies, the Government National Mortgage Association (Ginnie Mae), the Federal Home Loan Mortgage Association (Freddie Mac), and the Federal National Mortgage Association (Fannie Mae). Mortgage-backed securities are considered very safe. They are guaranteed by the issuer, and since they are made up of pools of mortgages, their return is not based on a single mortgage holder.

Risks and Benefits of purchasing residential MBS

Investing in MBS represents a low risk alternative to investing in other income funds such as a bond fund. For investors looking for a steady stream of income at a higher interest rate than most government bonds pay, mortgage-backed securities provide an appealing option. Provided the investor does not invest in a "private label" MBS and sticks with GNMA or FNMA MBS, the rewards are better than treasuries and the risk is only slightly higher. Mortgage-backed securities are ideal for investors interested in safety and income. Mortgage-backed securities would not be appropriate for investors interested in capital appreciation. "Private Label" MBS were sold in abundance pre-2008 by Wall Street firms. These MBS were securities that were backed by Sub-Prime and Alternative-A type of loans. In this chapter, we are not referring to investing in this type of MBS, as I have illustrated in the previous chapter that the underlying fundamentals of these type of loans were flawed and since very few investors today issue these loans, we won't explain in detail the "private label" MBS in this chapter.

Benefits

There are several important benefits of owning mortgage-backed securities. Safety and a steady stream of income are the most obvious, but there are some other benefits, as well, such as:

- **Excellent interest rates.** The interest they pay is higher than the rate offered by other government bonds and most investment grade corporate bonds.

- **Liquidity.** There is a huge secondary market for mortgage-backed securities, so you can buy and sell them whenever you wish. If you don't want to hold them through maturity, it's easy to find a buyer on the secondary market.
- **Easy to buy.** They are easy to buy and can be purchased through your bank or your broker.

Risks

Perhaps the biggest drawback to mortgage-backed securities is the uncertainty over how long they will continue to pay off. If you buy an MBS when interest rates are high, you might benefit with a good return for the 30-year term of the security. Unfortunately, if interest rates start to drop, you may be disappointed because homeowners are very likely to pay off their mortgages when interest rates fall. It would be just a matter of time before all of the borrowers in the pool will have refinanced and returned the principal. As a MBS owner, you would receive your principal back, and therefore, would no longer receive interest payments. This is not the end of the world for the investor, however the investor would have to look for a new place to invest in a lower interest rate market.

The opposite side of this scenario can be just as challenging for investors. If an investor buys an MBS when interest rates are low, and rates start to climb, homeowners are going to hold onto their old mortgages. The borrowers would not refinance into a higher rate as a result, MBS investors would be tied to those low rates for the full term of the security. This is bad if you the investor is stuck with a lower rate than he or she could earn if he or she could reinvest in the newer, higher-yielding MBS.

Mortgage-backed securities have some other minor drawbacks, as well:

- **Lower return than stocks**. Although mortgage-backed securities typically pay higher rates than other government bonds and AAA corporate bonds, they still fall well below average annual returns offered by stocks and high yield corporate bonds. But they are much safer than stocks or junk bonds.
- **Long term.** Many mortgage-backed securities are issued with maturities of up to 30 years, so you could be stuck with them for a long time. However, you can buy an MBS with a shorter term on the secondary

market, and you can unload your MBS on the secondary market whenever you wish.

- **High cost of admission**. If you want to buy a MBS from Ginnie Mae, the lowest-priced security you can purchase is $25,000. However, Freddie Mac and Fannie Mae securities are available in $1,000 increments.
- **Fully taxable**. Unlike government bonds, mortgage-backed securities are fully taxable by federal, state, and local governments.

Purchasing the MBS

You can buy mortgage-backed securities through most brokers. The fees are similar to bonds where you would pay between 0.5 and 2 percent, depending on the size of the bond and some other factors. Non-accredited investors can purchase MBS.

Ginnie Mae securities come in denominations of $25,000 and higher. Freddie Mac and Fannie Mae securities' minimum purchase denomination is only $1,000. You can buy MBS's on the secondary market with nearly any duration you want, but typically 15 or 30 year terms are purchased.

Investment Option #2 –Purchase Commercial Mortgage-Backed Securities

Commercial loans can also be pooled and sold as Commercial Mortgage-Backed Securities, or CMBS. Commercial mortgage-backed securities (CMBS) are a type of mortgage-backed security backed by commercial mortgages rather than residential real estate. CMBS tend to be more complex and volatile than residential mortgage-backed securities due to the unique nature of the underlying property assets.

CMBS issues are usually structured as multiple tranches, similar to collateralized mortgage obligations (CMOs), rather than typical residential "passthroughs." The typical structure for the securitization of commercial real estate loans is a real estate mortgage investment conduit or REMIC. A REMIC is a creation of the tax law that allows the trust to be a pass-through entity which is not subject to tax at the trust level. A REMIC is "an entity that holds a fixed pool of mortgages and issues multiple classes of interests in itself to investors" under U.S. Federal income tax law and is "treated like a partnership for Federal income tax purposes with its income passed through to its interest holders." REMICs are used for the pooling of mortgage loans and issuance of mortgage-backed securities and have been a key contributor to the success of the mortgage-backed securities market over the past several decades. CMBSs typically carry less prepayment risk than other MBS types. Commercial mortgages often contain lockout provisions after which they can be subject to defeasance, yield maintenance and prepayment penalties to protect bondholders.

Risks and benefits of purchasing Commercial MBS

Investing in CMBS represents a moderate risk alternative depending on the issuer and investing in other income funds such as a bond fund. Because of the structures of most CMBS are in a REMIC or trust, the trust breaks the pools down into tranches and sells them as bonds. Investors can purchase higher or lower rated bonds. Starting with AAA rated and down to Junk, CMBS bonds can have varying degrees of risk depending on the repayment position of the bond. The lower the grade of bond is, the higher the risk but also the higher the return. CMBS are likely a higher risk class than MBS secured by residential agency loans, because CMBS do not have the backing of the government.

Purchasing the MBS

Just like with residential MBS, you can buy mortgage-backed securities through most brokers. Non accredited investors can purchase CMBS. Consult your financial advisor for direction and details.

Investment Option # 3- Purchase Collateralized Mortgage Obligations

An investor can purchase another mortgage supported investment known as a CMO. A **collateralized mortgage obligation (CMO)** is a debt security that repackages and directs the payments of principal and interest from a collateral pool to different types and maturities of securities. CMOs were first created in 1983 by the investment banks Salomon Brothers and First Boston. A CMO is a debt security issued by a special purpose entity. The entity is the legal owner of a pool of mortgages. Investors in a CMO buy bonds issued by the entity, and they receive payments from the income generated by the mortgages according to a defined set of rules. The pool of mortgages are collateral and divided into classes that are similar in credit worthiness or other characteristics. These groups or classes are called tranches. Unlike traditional mortgage pass-through securities, CMOs feature different payment streams and risks, depending on investor preferences.

Risks and benefits of purchasing Collateralized Mortgage Obligations

Typically only institutional investors purchase CMO due to their complexity. For this reason we will not be digging deeper into this option but it is possible that your retirement account includes CMO's.

Investment Option # 4 – Invest in a Pool of Mortgages or a Mortgage Fund

For the investor that wants to invest in mortgages, but does not like the yields of the MBS, CMBS, and CMO markets, the non-traditional route could be an option to consider. As I have mentioned throughout this book, from what I have observed, most investors do not invest in mortgages and especially do not or have not ever invested in mortgage pools or a mortgage fund. One of the main reasons for this is that very few options to do so exist for the average investor. A mortgage pool or a mortgage fund spreads the investors' money over all the mortgages in the pool or fund, diversifying the risk should one or a few loans default. Exactly as investing in MBS or CMO, which are essentially mortgage pools, the investor should review exact loan characteristics that make up the loans in the pool or fund. When researching mortgage pools or mortgage funds, I found relatively few options. Private equity and hedge funds offer investors the ability to invest in mortgage pools or funds with varying options for the investor.

There are various reasons that investing in mortgage pools or mortgage funds is not prevalent in the investment world and I assume the list would include:

- Lack of knowledge by the investor
- Lack of awareness by the investor
- Very few mortgage pools or funds remain after 2008
- Most mortgage pools or funds are privately held and therefore not liquid
- Lack of transparency by the companies offering the pools or funds
- Most Registered Investment Advisors do not support this type of investment
- Many mortgage pools or funds are too small for most broker dealers to get comfortable investing.

Risks and benefits of investing in Mortgage Pools or Funds

As a mortgage fund manager and an experienced mortgage investor for 31 years, I believe that I am very biased with my answers on risks and benefits for investors who look to invest in mortgage pools or fund. Clearly I would not have written this book if I did not support this type of investment. The key to the argument is in the analyzing of the characteristics that make up the loans in the fund or pool. To generically say that "all loans" or "all loan pools" have the same risk would be a ridiculous statement. It would be like saying that all public companies or corporate bonds carry the same risk.

Risks

From my research, most mortgage pools or funds are private companies. The loans are not "agency eligible" or insured or guaranteed by the government, meaning the loans would be considered "private label." Most investors only have to think back to the 2008 meltdown that was partially brought on by lenders originating and selling "private label" mortgages and selling them to investors as safe investments or mortgage-backed securities. The key to evaluating the risk has to do with the underlying loan characteristics of the loans that secure the investors' capital. Regardless of the structure of the company or the fund that owns the pool of loans, the investor needs to review specifically the ownership structure of the underlying fund and the details of loan characteristics that make up the assets in the fund or pool. While we are sounding redundant, the investor who invests in pools when evaluating the risks should review the loan or fund documents when reviewing the risk associated with the investment. I have organized what aspects the investor should consider when investing in a mortgage pool or mortgage fund.

Investors should review:

- What security instrument is utilized by the company or fund in securing the investor
- The property types and characteristics that secure the loans in pool or fund.
- The borrower characteristics for the loans in pool or fund
- The geographic locations of the loans in the pool or fund
- The Loan-to-Value for the loans in the pool or fund
- The loan terms for loans in the pool or fund
- The management fees for the loan pool or fund manager
- The servicing practices of the manager of the pool or fund
- What lockup period or restrictions are there in getting investment returned.

- How much experience the fund manager has.
- How liquid the investment is in the fund.
- If non-accredited investors can invest in the pool or fund.

Benefits

The benefits of a fund or pool of mortgages is that it spreads the risk over many loans versus investing in just one mortgage loan. While a MBS and a CMBS does the same thing, the key benefit is to focus on what the fund or pool consists in and what specific collateral backs the loans. If there was market research on the average investor returns between a MBS, CMBS, and a mortgage fund, it would likely suggest that the investment returns on the mortgage fund would be higher, because it is likely the mortgage fund is invested in higher yielding mortgages as we mentioned earlier, like "private label" or "non-agency eligible" mortgages. Mortgages that are converted into securities are typically a better grade that a fund or a pool. Now, this statement is certainly not true of all funds or pools, but just an anecdotal statement about the comparisons of MBS, CMS and mortgage funds. When I get asked about the benefits of investing in the LYNK Capital fund, the fund that I am in charge of, I explain that it is an income fund that provides monthly income, at higher than market returns, where the investor's capital is secured by real estate assets. While this can likely be said of all mortgage backed securities, the LYNK fund produces over 7% higher annual returns than most mortgage backed securities.

PURCHASING INVESTMENTS IN LOAN POOLS OR FUNDS

The research I have completed does not provide clear data on how many loan pools or mortgage funds are available to investors. Investors that want to invest in mortgage loan pools or funds can locate companies and funds offering investors options to invest. Many of the private mortgage funds require investors to be accredited. The SEC has a section on the definition of what you an investor needs to do to qualify as an accredited investor but I have provided some highlights of this section below. This section is not meant to provide any legal advice on qualifying as an accredited investor.

SEC definition from SEC act of 1933, section 230

(a) Accredited investor. Accredited investor shall mean any person who comes within any of the following categories, or who the issuer reasonably believes comes within any of the following categories, at the time of the sale of the securities to that person:

(1) Any bank as defined in section 3(a)(2) of the Act, or any savings and loan association or other institution as defined in section 3(a)(5)(A) of the Act whether acting in its individual or fiduciary capacity; any broker or dealer registered pursuant to section 15 of the Securities Exchange Act of 1934; any insurance company as defined in section 2(a)(13) of the Act; any investment company registered under the Investment Company Act of 1940 or a business development company as defined in section 2(a)(48) of that Act; any Small Business Investment Company licensed by the U.S. Small Business Administration under section 301(c) or (d) of the Small Business Investment Act of 1958; any plan established and maintained by a state, its political subdivisions, or any agency or instrumentality of a state or its political subdivisions, for the benefit of its employees, if such plan has total assets in excess of $5,000,000; any employee benefit plan within the meaning of the Employee Retirement Income Security Act of 1974 if the investment decision is made by a plan fiduciary, as defined in section 3(21) of such act, which is either a bank, savings and loan association, insurance company, or registered investment adviser, or if the employee benefit plan has total assets in excess of $5,000,000 or, if a self-directed plan, with investment decisions made solely by persons that are accredited investors;

(2) Any private business development company as defined in section 202(a)(22) of the Investment Advisers Act of 1940;

(3) Any organization described in section 501(c)(3) of the Internal Revenue Code, corporation, Massachusetts or similar business trust, or partnership, not formed for the specific purpose of acquiring the securities offered, with total assets in excess of $5,000,000;

(4) Any director, executive officer, or general partner of the issuer of the securities being offered or sold, or any director, executive officer, or general partner of a general partner of that issuer;

(5) Any natural person whose individual net worth, or joint net worth with that person's spouse, exceeds $1,000,000.

(i) Except as provided in paragraph (a)(5)(ii) of this section, for purposes of calculating net worth under this paragraph (a)(5):

(A) The person's primary residence shall not be included as an asset;

(B) Indebtedness that is secured by the person's primary residence, up to the estimated fair market value of the primary residence at the time of the sale of securities, shall not be included as a liability (except that if the amount of such indebtedness outstanding at the time of sale of securities exceeds the amount outstanding 60 days before such time, other than as a result of the acquisition of the primary residence, the amount of such excess shall be included as a liability); and

(C) Indebtedness that is secured by the person's primary residence in excess of the estimated fair market value of the primary residence at the time of the sale of securities shall be included as a liability;

(ii) Paragraph (a)(5)(i) of this section will not apply to any calculation of a person's net worth made in connection with a purchase of securities in accordance with a right to purchase such securities, provided that:

(A) Such right was held by the person on July 20, 2010;

(B) The person qualified as an accredited investor on the basis of net worth at the time the person acquired such right; and

(C) The person held securities of the same issuer, other than such right, on July 20, 2010.

(6) Any natural person who had an individual income in excess of $200,000 in each of the two most recent years or joint income with that person's spouse in excess of $300,000 in each of those years and has a reasonable expectation of reaching the same income level in the current year;

(7) Any trust, with total assets in excess of $5,000,000, not formed for the specific purpose of acquiring the securities offered, whose purchase is directed by a sophisticated person as described in §230.506(b)(2)(ii); and

SUMMARY OF MORTGAGE
INVESTMENT OPTIONS FOR INVESTORS

- **MBS** - MBS produce better returns than treasuries but carry a slightly higher risk of investment than treasuries. They have lower yields than mortgage pools or fund.

- **CMBS** - Investing in CMBS requires clarity in knowing what makes up the underlying mortgages and the characteristics of the underwriting and the real estate securing the investment in order to properly gauge investment risk.

- **CMO** - CMO are likely not a good option for most investors due to their complexity so I am not going to discuss them further in this chapter.

- **Mortgage Pools or Funds** – Non-accredited investors may not be able to take advantage of many of the mortgage funds or pools that invest in high yielding mortgages. Most of the private mortgage funds that I know of require the investor to be accredited so this is even more reason that for many investors, investing in mortgages is not a viable activity, at least until this book explains how to make it a viable activity.

Comparison of Real Estate, Stock Market, and Mortgage Investments
In this section of the chapter we will review the last 100 years or as much data as we can to compare investments in three of the most common investment vehicles alongside investing in mortgages.

REAL ESTATE VS. STOCK MARKET

Many make the argument that more money can be made in the stock market than through real estate investments. There is an overwhelming amount of data that can support this argument and likely a similar amount of data that can support the opposite. Depending on what time frame you review, the numbers can be dramatically different. But, for the purposes of this exercise, let's take a look at trends over the past 100 years.

In the graph below, notice that the trends over the past 100 years of housing and the stock market, have increased at "relatively" similar paces, with appreciation higher in the stock market versus the real estate market. Granted, both have had upticks and downturns, but the overall trends have been favorable. The one problem with this graph is that it has data through 2010. In writing this book in 2015, my portfolio of real estate has performed well since 2010 and my investments in the stock market have been stagnant.

What appears to be evident is the stock market has been more volatile, while the housing market has been more stable. You may notice that when the stock market fell, housing remained relatively stable. Likewise, in the real estate decline of 2008, the stock market experienced a quicker rebound. The point of this illustration is that diversifying investments between the stock market and real estate can be a very sound strategy. Stocks help your portfolio grow while real estate provides both a hedge against inflation and a low 'correlation' to stocks – in other words, it may rise when stocks fall. Because real estate investments move at such a different pace than other investments, they can actually help stabilize the overall returns of your portfolio. Consider the chart below from Case Shiller. It illustrates the variations from the Dow Jones, Standard and Poor's, Nasdaq markets and the real estate market from January

2000 to January 2012. An investor that began in this period would have performed better owning real estate than stocks.

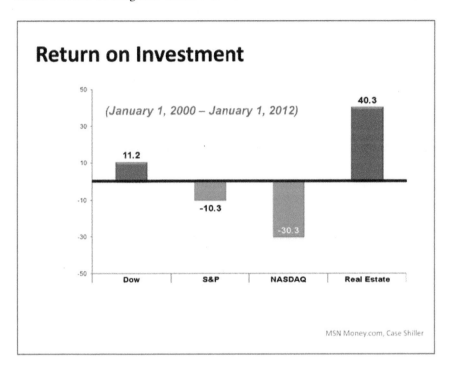

Comparison of Mortgages vs. Treasuries

The chart below represents 10-year treasury Yields from 1962. We discuss in this book the target interest rate that an investor should charge is no less than 3-5% over the 10 year Treasury. While the Treasuries represent safe investments backed by the government, mortgage returns can produce better yields. If invested in GNMA or FNMA mortgage-backed securities the yields would typically be 1-3% higher than the 10 year treasuries. Throughout this book, my objective is to convince the reader to consider investing in commercial mortgages, either as a private lender or as an investor in mortgage funds.

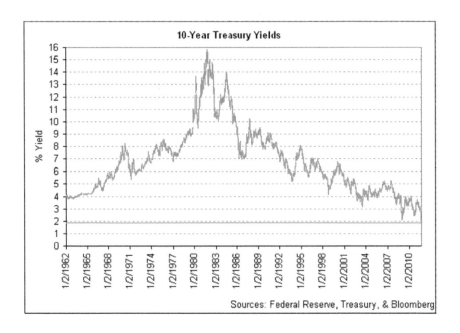

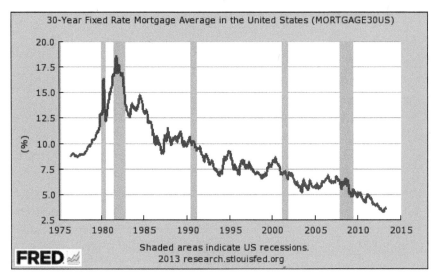

Summary on investing in Stocks, Real Estate, and Mortgages

The Dow Jones has produced about 4.8% average annual appreciation since 1900 and the real estate appreciation has been approximately 3.7%. Neither of these figures include dividends or income, but are simply the average appreciated annual amount. The estimated average annual rate on the 10 year us treasuries since 1900 has been approximately 4.9%. This book is not about me giving you investment advice, but more about my providing an argument that a portion of an investor's assets should be in mortgages. Mortgages are a fixed income asset that typically provides a non-correlated strategy to equities. My last point here is that in my 31-year career as a lender, I have been able to achieve 3-10% over the 10-year treasury returns. For this main reason, I have argued that lending money on a risk-adjusted return is as good, if not better, investment as anything else offered today and in past years.

In Other Words

- ❖ Mortgage investments are a secured fixed income alternative.
- ❖ There are relatively only a handful of various options to invest in mortgages that include MBS, CMBS, CMO, mortgage loan pools, mortgage funds.
- ❖ MBS are liquid as they are typically publically traded.
- ❖ CMBS can be liquid but vary based on each issue.
- ❖ A smart investor researches the characteristics that make up a mortgage loan pool or fund.
- ❖ Targeted yields on "private label" loan pools or funds are typically higher than most MBS and CMBS options.
- ❖ The historical returns on equities have outperformed those of the real estate; however more volatility has existed in the equity markets versus the real estate markets.
- ❖ Mortgage pools or private mortgage lending can produce returns that are greater by 3-10 percentage points than 10-year treasuries, however, much greater risk exists.

BE THE BANK:

Chapter 4:
Knowing what to Ask when Investing in Mortgages

Are you are ready to get an education on mortgage investing?

HERE'S WHAT WE COVER IN THIS CHAPTER

- What the goal of every mortgage lender or investor is.
- What key questions all mortgage investors need to know.
- Key attributes of mortgage: property types, mortgage types, geographic areas, loan size parameters, and many more keys to mortgage lending
- Loan guidelines, loan to value restrictions, payment and affordability, and basics of borrower credit profiles
- Why and how the borrower must benefit from borrowing from the lender.
- Chapter summary

Before we jump into a very long chapter I wanted to point out to the reader and hopeful mortgage investor that we use "lender" often in this chapter and throughout the book. When we refer to "lender" we are using this synonymous with "investor" meaning that the lender is potentially you as the mortgage loan investor.

In the previous two chapters we have briefly discussed mortgage investing with a relative overview and historical perspective of mortgages and investing including details of the different types of mortgages. In this chapter we will explore details of mortgage lending and especially if you are looking to invest in individual mortgages or mortgage loan pools. To clarify what we mean by a mortgage loan pool, a loan pool refers to a group of loans that can be structured as a fund or simply a group of loans where your investment is secured by the group. If you are investing in a mortgage loan fund, the fund owns the mortgages and by way of your ownership in the fund, you, the investor would own a percentage of the underlying mortgage loans. Regardless of investing in an individual loan or a loan pool an investor needs to know how to determine the characteristics, loan quality and risk profile of the loan or loans securing the investment.

While banks and non-banks that originate mortgage loans under the "held for investment group" differ in many ways in how they originate or invest their mortgage loans, there are many common goals between them. These goals are likely consistent with any mortgage investors' goals. Your goal, my goal and the bank's goals are all likely the same and that is *"to lend money secured by the real estate to a borrower that benefits from the use of the money and repays the capital advanced with the required interest or return on the capital."*

To really drive this point home, below is my goal as private mortgage investor:

"My goal as mortgage investor is to lend money secured by real estate to a borrower that benefits from the use of the money and repays the capital advanced by me with the required return on the invested capital in the time frame agreed upon, where the risk of loss of the capital is well protected by securing the real estate."

Given the goals outlined for all banks and non-banks, including my goal, a smart lender or investor should ask some basic questions on every mortgage investment decision.

As a general overview, it would be impossible to publish how each and every mortgage lender, mortgage banker, and mortgage loan investor determines how to evaluate the risks associated with mortgage lending. As a general rule, all banks and non-banks review a handful of the same guidelines before originating or investing as a mortgage lender and providing a mortgage loan. I want all readers of this book who are interested in becoming a private mortgage investor/ lender to consider some key questions. The "core" elements or perhaps "questions" that all banks and non-banks consider are the same ones that you and I, as an investor in mortgages should consider, and these are:

1. What is the right type of loan for my investment risk tolerance?
2. What is the right property type for my investment risk tolerance?
3. In what geographic area should I lend?
4. What (LTV) loan-to-value and marketability requirements should I require?
5. What credit and income requirements should I require when I am evaluating the borrower profile?
6. For what period do I want my mortgage investment to be loaned?
7. What interest rate of return should I charge or earn for the corresponding risk?
8. How well is my principal investment protected by the real estate collateral?
9. Is the mortgage loan providing a benefit to the borrower?
10. What are the required mortgage loan size amount minimums and maximums?
11. Does the mortgage loan comply with all state and federal laws?

So now we have identified some of the key elements or questions that need to be known and clearly understood before any investor, bank or non-bank, participates in mortgage lending or decides to invest in mortgages. Let's look at each key area or question and hopefully provide you with the basic knowledge of why the question is important and what you as a new investor in mortgages should do to maximize your investment and manage the risks associated with investing in mortgages.

<u>Key question #1</u> – What is the right "type" of loan for my investment risk tolerance.

In chapter two we listed the different mortgage types and briefly described each type. To better assist the reader, we will re-list the mortgage types in this section but instead of describing what it is as in chapter two, we will provide a statement of why an investor should or should not invest in this type of loan and provide a brief explanation on the risks associated with investing in the specific loan type. At the end of the list there will be my conclusion on what a mortgage investor should consider specific to the mortgage type.

Mortgage Types

- *First Mortgages* – Very good idea for investor to be secured by the real estate as a first lien on the property.

- *Second Mortgages* –Typically, a bad idea to be the investor that is secured behind a first mortgage unless the combined loan to value (CLTV) is below 60%. Even if the LTV is below 60%, being in a 2nd position behind a 1st mortgage, this adds a level of additional risk to your investment. I would not suggest providing 2nd mortgages unless you are seasoned mortgage investor.

- *Credit Lines* – Not a good idea. Only a bad idea because the lender has to be prepared to service the loan advances and the principal pay downs by the borrower as often as the borrower draws down on the line and repays the line. This could be a real pain and could create a ton of work for a private investor making mortgage loans.

- *Closed End Mortgages* – Good idea. This type of loan allows it to have a defined due date with no ability for the borrower to re-advance principal of the loan once paid down. The majority of all mortgage are closed end.

- *Fixed Rates vs. Variable Rates mortgage loans* – Both fixed and variable rates are good for an investment if the interest rate that is fixed provides a high enough rate that the investor is happy during the entire term of the loan. If an investor makes a 10 year fixed rate loan at 10% interest, the investor has to live with earning the 10% for the entire 10 years. The benefit of an adjustable rate loan is that if the prevailing interest rates increase in the overall marketplace, the rate you charge to the borrower can increase. The bad news is about variable rate loans is the investor has to insure that the borrower is properly informed at each interest rate adjustment. The most common adjustable rate loan is tied to the Wall Street Journal Prime Rate that gets published each day. My advice to investors that are considering a mortgage investment lasting more than 3-5 years should have the mortgage type be an adjustable rate loan versus a fixed rate loan.

- *Interest only mortgage loans* – Good idea. This type of loan is easy to service and keeps the borrower's payments lower as a result of no principal being applied to the loan payment each month. Some would argue this is bad because the borrower is not reducing the balance with each payment, but in the majority of cases the investor reading this book will be investing in short term loans anyway so having the loan payments as interest only will not have any material effect on borrower or investors.

- *Amortizing mortgage loan* – Not really good or bad. I do not recommend this type of mortgage. A private investor might not want the hassle of keeping track of an amortizing loan; however the benefit to both borrower and investor is that the principal balance of the loan is reducing each month. If a private investor is planning to make long term loans, meaning loans longer than five years than making the loans amortize makes sense. Shorter term loans should be interest only for both the investor's and borrower's benefit.

- *Balloon payment provision* – Good idea for investor. My advice to most investors looking to invest in mortgages is to lend short term. The longest term an investor should consider is five years but ideally three years or less if best. The purpose of a "balloon" feature in a mortgage is so the lender/investor can renegotiate the terms should the investor choose. Often market conditions change and the lender/investor wants to have the ability to change the terms when or if the market conditions warrant.

- *Commercial mortgage loans* – Very good idea. We will discuss in this book that an investor <u>ONLY</u> wants to originate and fund loans that fall outside the consumer lending laws. Loans that are commercial in nature are much less restrictive to all parties and provide the flexibility to the borrower and investor that a mortgage to a consumer does not provide. We will discuss more about consumer vs. commercial mortgages later in the book.

- *Residential or consumer mortgage loans* – Very bad idea. Consumer laws require too many lending requirements that most private investors will not want to comply with. These types of loans are best left to the banks and mortgage companies.

- *Construction or renovation mortgage loans* – Typically a good idea. This is a good idea if the mortgage investor either has construction experience or has turned over the investment to an experienced fund manager. One of the benefits to investors is that borrowers that have a need for renovation or construction money are typically willing to pay a premium for the use of the money. A higher degree of risk is associated with renovation and construction lending. The LYNK capital fund focuses on these type of mortgage loans specifically to maximize the return to the fund.

- *Bridge mortgage loans* – Typically a good idea. Bridge loans typically allow an over-collateralizing to the mortgage investor and this type of loan provides a great benefit to the borrower because it immediately increases the amount of cash available to him.

- *Blanket loans* – Typically a good idea. The same concept as bridge loans. Borrower is providing an over-collateralization for an investor by securing multiple properties. Blanket loans are not very common in the mainstream lending industry but this lending practice allows for a private lender to capitalize on this unique loan structure.

Loan Type summary and advice

With so many different types of mortgages how should an investor, especially a novice investor determine what type or types of loans are best to invest in? My advice is usually the same to all investors regardless of much else.

"To invest ONLY *1st lien mortgages* structured as a *Commercial loan,* as *interest only*, balloon *loan* where the balance is due in less than 3 years. I allow the loan to be on one property or multiple properties (blanket or bridge loan) for the purposes of acquisition, cash out, *renovation, construction* or any purpose that provides a clear borrower benefit."

Key question #2 – What is the right "property type" for my investment risk tolerance?

Anyone considering investing in mortgages either an individual loan, as a pool or loans, or a fund should determine what type of property or properties are being used as collateral. All banks and non-banks lend on specific property types. It is not typical of most lenders or mortgage investors to lend on *ALL* the property types available to lend on. Property types can vary drastically so a lender and investor should become familiar with all the property types. Mistakes can be made by a novice investor by lending on the most challenging property types such as a golf course, restaurant or special use property. It is not to say that these specialty or single use properties cannot properly secure an investor's mortgage but should the investor have to foreclose on this type of property, it could be more difficult to sell the property. Each investor must make a determination as to which property types suit them the best. The property types listed below represent a majority of the real estate property types. There are, however, many additional property types that may be considered.

Property Types

- *Single Family Residential* – one dwelling unit on one parcel of land. This property type can be owner occupied, a second home or a rental property. This property type is the most commonly known property type.

- *Multi-Family Residential* – multiple dwelling units on one parcel of land. This is an apartment building or any single structure that has more than one living unit.

- *Mixed Use* – two or more different uses for one improved property. (Example: a retail storefront on the first floor with 3 rental apartments above it.)

- *Industrial Zoned* – A property that can only be used for approved industrial type businesses. Residential or office uses are not permitted. This property type is often used for manufacturing.

- *Commercial Office* – Used for business and offices purposes.

- *Commercial Retail* – Utilized for retail business such as storefront or retail business.

- *Senior Housing* – Used for persons 55 and older. Can also include medical related accommodations such as continuing care, skilled nursing or assisted living.

- *Special or Single Purpose* - can include churches, gas stations, funeral homes, golf courses, hotels, etc. In the special or single purpose property type this typically requires an operating business to generate income for the property owner.

Property Type summary and advice

Investors that are ready to make mortgage investments should review the list of property types and identify the types that best suits their background or comfort levels. Some investors prefer industrial properties, while others prefer only apartments as collateral for their loans. This is not an area of better or worse but the mortgage investor must be knowledgeable about the property type that secures their investment.

Key question # 3 – In what geographic area should I lend?

Geographic Areas

As you would assume, this question asks in what geographic areas you as a lender want to invest or lend. All banks and non-banks have a defined lending area.

For example, most community banks only lend in markets in which they have local offices or branch locations. This is a good approach to lending. Having knowledge of the local real estate community and/or the economy can provide good information when investing and making loan decisions. Personal knowledge of the demographics and other indicators can provide intelligence that an out-of-town lender may not have.

For the reader who is expecting to be his or her own private lender, I would suggest that you lend in your immediate community at the beginning and expand once you gain experience. Lenders typically choose certain markets based on the market demographics. For example, there is a vast difference between a lender making loans in rural communities vs. urban communities. There is a vast difference between the real estate markets of Deltona Florida vs. Orlando Florida yet they are only 25 minutes away from each other. If I were not familiar with both of these locations in Florida, I could make a big mistake on valuations and marketability. We will discuss valuations and marketability in later chapters.

Geographic area summary and advice

The mortgage investor should consider only lending in areas in which they have knowledge in and can conveniently visit the property in the event the mortgage has to be foreclosed on. The rule of thumb that I employ is the farther away from the core lending areas that one is familiar with, the lower the loan-to-value and the higher the return should be. The LYNK Capital fund that I manage only lends in 6 states in the southeast where I have been lending for many years and where our staff resides and where we have knowledge of the markets.

Key question # 4 – What loan to value and marketability requirements should I require?

Understanding Value and Marketability

When a lender, regardless of bank or non-bank, is evaluating a potential mortgage, determining the value of the collateral and more specifically what percentage of the value (LTV) should be loaned becomes one of the most critical aspects of the entire process. It is common sense to say that if a lender or private investor lends too much to a borrower who defaults, the investor could lose money from the sale of the asset used as collateral. In the previous chapter we stated that one of the requirements to successful mortgage investing is that the collateral utilized to secure the capital ALWAYS needs to protect the capital invested. So let's explore what steps have we taken to protect the capital, in the event of a loan default.

To be clear, collateral is something that is pledged as a security for repayment of a mortgage loan, to be forfeited in the event of a default by the borrower. A lender must be able to determine the fair market value of the collateral, prior to the loan closing, and its potential value throughout the term of the loan. Sure, it is easy to say that the lender should determine the value of the property at the time the loan is made, but the lender also should have indicators of future value to determine the likelihood that this property will either appreciate or depreciate in value. There is no magic wand, but there are a few formulas that can greatly reduce loan losses in the event of a loan default.

A lender or investor should understand that value is somewhat of a subjective figure that varies based on market supply and demand, along with a variety of other influencing factors. To determine value, a lender should take into consideration:

- The Value Range
- Marketability of the Property
- Highest & Best Use of the Property

What is The Value Range?

I often get asked what value you are placing on this particular property. I then reply: "I am not sure the exact value but the range is probably x on the low end and y on the high end." My approach to value and ultimately safe property valuations is based on understanding that the value of your collateral is <u>not</u> a fixed number, but rather a "**value range**", one that moves based on supply and demand, economic conditions at the time of sale, availability of credit, and other factors. To thoroughly understand the value range, it is recommended that two to three data sources or different opinions be considered. The most common way to determine value is to hire an appraiser. The appraiser should be state-licensed or have other certification. If they are a member of a professional organization such as The Appraisal Foundation, they will adhere to certain ethics codes and rules of conduct. If they are a member of such an organization, they will be less likely to adjust the assessment value of the property appraisal according to personal interests.

In addition to utilizing certified appraisers, some lenders have additional requirements for the appraiser. For example, at the mortgage fund I oversee, we require the appraiser to live or work within 30 miles of the subject property. We believe this helps to ensure that the individual who is evaluating the market value of the property has a basic understanding of the real estate market in which the property is located. While it may be challenging, particularly in rural areas to meet this requirement, we believe this prerequisite helps us understand the overall familiarity the individual may or may not have with an area and even helps us determine if additional opinions should be requested. Keep in mind that the job of the appraiser is to provide an estimated value of the property based on the value of local real estate, property location and its particular amenities and the overall condition of the property. However, an appraisal does not always identify what I call marketability factors. For this reason, a smart lender will also seek out the opinion of local real estate agents and/or auctioneers to assist in providing data and opinions of value range.

In addition to the above, and perhaps regardless of their opinions, a smart lender will always perform a site inspection and visit the collateral being used in the mortgage investment. A site inspection allows a private investor to verify and validate all the information that is provided by the third parties such as realtor opinion of value or appraiser. A site inspection has more to do with fraud protection and the property marketability assessment than value. We will discuss marketability in further detail, in just a moment. Keep in mind that for today's nationwide banks and non-banks, a site visit from the lender is often not practical. This is certainly a contributing factor to the reason many banks and lenders have fallen prey to fraud and other real estate schemes. But, for community banking or most private lending companies, the lender is typically operating in a defined geographic area. This is not only smart, but an investor should be concerned about making mortgage investment or investing in a mortgage fund where a site visit by the investor is NOT performed. In other words, as a private mortgage investor, don't invest in a company or lend on a property you don't personally see or can see.

Ultimately, the lender must be educated and experienced enough in the market to develop a final value range on which the loan will be based upon. The crash of 2008 was overrun with inexperienced lenders, appraisers and other real estate "professionals" who were accepting inflated values and violating many of the basic principles of lending. This created a lending climate that allowed terrible decision making and financially tragic circumstances to occur.

Now, let's consider how a property's value range should help guide the lending decision. Consider the following property scenario, which is based on a real life loan example, where I personally invested and eventually had to foreclose on the property. Notice the potential impact to the value of a property and factors.

Date of Appraisal	Appraised Value	Value Range	Factors
2005	$210,000	$180-230k	Market demand is high. Bidding wars are occurring on homes. Interest rates are moderate; money is accessible to borrowers
2008-09	$150,000	$135-165k	Three years later, the market has substantially declined, the economy is contracted, housing inventories are high, and demand for housing is low.
2011-12	$175,000	$160-190k	The housing market is recovering, interest rates are at all-time lows, financing is available, but still somewhat stringent.
2014-15	$200,000	$180-$220k	The housing market has 'rebounded', values are increasing, housing inventory is low, financing is readily available and guidelines are loosening.

In each date described above, the appraised value could have a **value range** of +/-10%. Now, let's consider how the value range factors into the critical decision regarding loan-to-value.

Another way to describe the value range is that under poor market conditions, the value will be at the low end and under strong market conditions at the high end.

Let's briefly explain LTV or loan-to-value because this is the term most often used in the lending industry. The loan-to-value (LTV) ratio is a financial term used by lenders to express the ratio of a loan to the value of an asset. The term is commonly used in the lending industry to represent the ratio of the first mortgage lien as a percentage of the total appraised value of real property. The concept is pretty simple. By using the value range of the property and applying some basic calculations, we can identify the low and high LTV range. Making decisions based on the range vs one figure improves the odds of reducing principle loss by the lender.

Think back to 2008 and the years that led up to it. Lenders were lending up to 125% of value. In many cases, the value was also inflated. Demand was so high, borrowers were in bidding wars and paying way more than the house was "valued." So, when the market went south, many homeowners (and lenders) had debt that far exceeded the actual property values.

Now, let's apply two LTV range concepts to help mitigate this risk even when real estate markets contract and values fall. These two simple rules can often insulate a **private lender or investor** and protect the principal investment.

My Rule #1:   lend 60% of the high end of the value range
                     Example: $210,000 x 60% = $126,000

My Rule #2:   lend up to 80% of the low end of the value range
                     Example: $150,000 x 80% = $120,000

Value Range: The value range in the above example is $150,000 -$210,000 & the targeted safe loan range is from $120,000 to $126,000

Now, let's refer to the chart below, using the same example and data provided earlier. You can see how each lender's risk could be increased or decreased, based upon the LTV, as the market changes. Lender A in the example is the only lender that does not have the principal investment or loan impacted by market changes because Lender A had a 40% cushion of value fluctuation. In addition, Lender A always maintains enough of a cushion to cover the costs of foreclosure and/or any marketability issues that may arise.

By contrast, lender B & C are both at risk of losing principal, depending upon marketability, economic and other influencing factors.

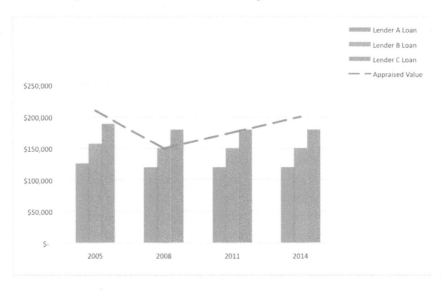

Lenders must interpret and predict property valuation and be able to mitigate risk based on the future "value range" of the property.

Now, let's consider other factors that affect and impact value.

Marketability

Marketability is the likelihood that the underlying real estate utilized as collateral for the loan will sell based on certain market conditions. Marketability can also be market appeal. The definition of marketability is "*A measure of the ability of something (in this case, a real estate property), to be bought and sold.*" If there is an active marketplace for a property, it has good marketability. Marketability plays a role in determining the property's liquidity except that liquidity implies that the value of the property is preserved whereas marketability simply indicates how easily something can be bought and sold.

Under ideal conditions, or in a best case scenario, the property securing the investment would be presented in move-in condition, market conditions would be favorable, with low housing inventory creating a high demand and borrowers would have easy access to loan programs and favorable interest rates. These conditions would create <u>high marketability</u> and generally bring the highest sales price possible for the property.

In a worst case scenario, the property is in foreclosure and may require major repairs or renovation. The housing inventories may be high with low buyer demand, and financing programs may not be readily available to borrowers and/or interest rates may be high. You may need to sell the property at a discount or at an auction just to move it. These conditions would create low marketability and bring the lowest sales price. I like to explain that value and marketability likely are related whereas one effects the other.

Marketability reflects how the market will react or respond to acquiring the property at any given point in time. Basically it is a "time" element of marketplace and specifically sale of the property. This would affect how long you may have to hold on to or maintain a property before it is sold at a reasonable price. Marketability is an important factor to consider because if you ever have to foreclose the property you will want to factor in its marketability since this will be a cost that must be borne by the lender. In mortgage investing, determining the marketability is as important as market value. Appraisers do include the marketing timeline for the sale of a property on most appraisals but unless an investor factors this timeline into the value range the investor could be utilizing a too high value range.

A story about marketability and value

I was on vacation in Puerto Rico with my family and a deal was emailed to me. Bank of America was owed $970,000 on this home and they were willing to sell me the debt for $315,000. The property was 4100 square feet, almost brand new, and was situated 2 blocks from the beach. The purchase price at $315,000 was 65/foot for this almost new 8 bedroom home. This price was less for the home than the previous owner paid for just the lot. I thought I stole the property at 65/foot. It would have cost me 120/foot just to re-build it. I bought the property a few days later while still on vacation. Here I was, paying 30% of what the bank was owed and less than 65/foot for this home 2 blocks from the ocean. I thought I got a good deal. When I finally went to see the property and performed my site inspection. I immediately went "oh shit", the layout of the interior of the home was dysfunctional and I knew that that this would have a definite impact on marketability and ultimately the sale price or value. Buyers that see this home will conclude the same. The point of this story is that homes in that market were selling for 120 per foot and it would have been easy for comparables (comps) to support this figure. It is also very likely that an appraiser would not have focused on the dysfunctional layout of the property and created a solid argument with comps that had better floor-plans. This would have distorted the real marketability and likely the value. While I may not have accurately identified the exact value range, my site in-spection, prior to investing, would have identified this issue.

Value and Marketability summary and advice

The investor needs to make sure the property value always protects the principal investment. This can normally be achieved by keeping the loan-to-value below 65% of the value of the secured asset. Utilize a value range and never exceed 80-85% of the low end and 65-70% of the high end of the value range. In ad-dition to value, personally inspect the property to evaluate the timeline or mar-ketability of the asset. If you are not managing the individual mortgages yourself and are relying on a fund manager or others, ask them if someone that is making the loan decisions is personally visiting the property utilized as collateral to fur-ther protect against risk of value and marketability. More will be discussed about LTV and site inspection in the chapter on mortgage loan underwriting.

Key question #5 – What credit and income requirements should I re-quire for my risk tolerance?

Credit (character) Parameters

In this section we will briefly discuss the role a borrower's credit plays in mak-ing mortgage loans. All lenders determine the acceptable credit parameters that their borrowers must meet to qualify for loans. These are typically out-lined in the lender's underwriting guidelines and formal policies and proce-dures. Regulated banks especially, MUST adhere to these written credit policies. All regulated lenders must review a borrower's credit history and willingness to repay the loan. Most banks and non-banks require the minimum credit standards to reflect very good credit. The days of lenders making loans to borrowers with poor credit are mostly a thing of the past. As a private lender who plans to invest in mortgage loans, it is good for you to learn the low and high credit spectrums to consider either as an individual who is going to make loans or if you are evaluating a fund or pool of loans. The key question to ask is what "credit profiles" or "credit scores" are required to allow loan approval. When I am teaching loan underwriters about credit I explain to them that the credit report history tells a story about character and historically a credit profile can often predict the risk of future payment default. It is certainly not the only indicator of default but it is one of several key determiners of default.

Profile description	Credit history description	Credit score range	Risk of default
Horrible credit profile	Entire history of bad credit	Below 580	Extremely high
Bad credit profile	Mostly bad history	558-620	High
Fair credit profile	Some bad and some good history	620-660	Possible
Good credit profile	Mostly good history	660-720	Not likely
Excellent credit profile	All good history	720 or higher	Not likely

We will discuss credit review in more detail in the chapter on underwriting. For the purposes of this chapter let's review the chart below, where I make a generic statement about a borrower's credit profile.

Income (affordability) parameters

Similar to credit guidelines, all lenders have policies and procedures surrounding the loan affordability by borrowers. Affordability simply means that the borrower can afford the new loan payments based on current monthly obligations or debts. The underwriting guidelines and policies of banks and non-banks specifically state the required documentation and affordability ratios for all loans considered. The guidelines set a standard list of the borrower income documents to prove they can afford to make the payments. In this section of this chapter we will not go into how to calculate affordability, but we will discuss how a private lender needs to understand the options available for consideration. Similar to the credit chart there should be an affordability chart to consider. Not all lenders use an affordability chart because they publish guidelines that state if a borrower is above the chart they qualify and if they are below they don't. My philosophy is more subjective because once again I use a range of affordability in making decisions vs a chart that says yes or no. We will cover this in more detail in the Underwriting chapter.

Affordability description	Affordability depth	Risk of default
Below 50% of expense coverage	Entire history documented poorly	Extremely high
50-100% of expense coverage	Recent history documented poorly	High
100-125% of expense coverage	Fluctuating history but sufficient	Somewhat high
Above 125% of expense coverage	Consistent and well documented history	Low

Credit and Income requirements summary and advice

Credit is the character of the borrower and income really means the affordability of the borrower when repaying money. Prior to closing a mortgage loan or investing in mortgage pools, the investor should know the profiles of the borrower's specific to *"character" and "affordability."* Understanding a borrower's character and affordability allows the investor to better **predict** the risk of default and better evaluate risk-based pricing. In the mortgage fund that I run, character and affordability drive the risk of default and investment returns, but we do allow for marginal credit profiles provided we are over-collateralized. It is not easy for the novice investor to inherently know one's character or predict default, as this typically comes from experience; however we hope to provide all our readers with the tools and framework to ask the right questions and interpret the answers and information.

Key question #6: For what period do I want my mortgage investment to be loaned?

All investors should consider the question of how long am I making this investment for and when do I want to be repaid for my capital. Many investors that I know do not ask this question because they hand over their hard-earned savings to investment advisors who formulate a plan based on retirement age. Nothing wrong with this concept, however when we are making investments we should always consider certain variables. Investing in any sector, regardless of what it is, has a cycle. Cycles to me are similar to the concept of bull or bear markets, recessions or expansions of the economy, inflation or deflation, appreciation or depreciation, and so on. I often lecture about the *4 seasons of investing* when there is a time to plant, a time to water and nurture the crops, a time to harvest, and a time to sell the crops. To me being a lender has risks that move with the variations of the seasons or cycles. Look at the banking world in the past 30 years and you can easily understand when banks were doing great and when banks were going under. Each time the economy contracted banks and other investors who were highly leveraged got squeezed. Anyway, I will stop here and just explain that every investor has to decide that they will ride out the cycles for the LONG haul or plan to invest for the period of time during the best time of the cycle. After 31 years of investing in real estate, mortgages, equities, and many businesses I chose to, at age 50, I to keep my mortgage investments short term. Short term means to me 3 years or less. Each investor can determine his or her investment period tolerance to determine the best term of his or her mortgage investment. I would offer advice that many commercial banks follow and that is to make one year loans that can renew each year, based on the lenders decision and adjustment to the economy.

Loan term summary and advice

Lend short term for 2-3 years or less to reduce interest rate or default risk. That's it, not much more advice to give.

Key question #7: What interest rate or rate of return should I earn for my risk?

You are probably reading this book because you want to benefit from my favorite investing strategy of lending money secured by real estate. The reason I have become an advocate of this alternative investing class is that I can easily argue and justify the risk with the associated return on the investment. Investing with tangible collateral at a defined return appeals to me. So what is the proper rate of return for investing in mortgages? This is a good question and one for which I am not sure what the correct answer may be. I would assume supply and demand would drive the balance between return on investment and risk, but for most of my career, private mortgage investing has produced annual returns that were substantially over most of the other markets and market benchmarks. We can review this question throughout this book, but for this chapter lets argue that as a private mortgage investor you should charge and earn 500-1,000 basis points over the 10 year US treasuries. That's 5-10 percentage points over the 10 year treasuries which at the time of writing were at 3.25%, therefore the average private lender should charge between 8.25-13.25%.

Interest rate of return advice

Rate of return as a private investor should be no less than 3% and as high as 10% over the 10-year treasury rate. Interest rate should be based on variables of risk as determined by you, the investor.

Key question #8: How well is my principal investment protected by the collateral?

All investing has capital risk. Smart investors know how to protect the downside risk and investing in mortgages is the same as other investing. So how does a mortgage lender or investor protect his or her capital? This is a question that has multiple answers and many bankers would argue: *"The loan that always performs never causes losses of investors' money."* All of us as bankers do our best to predict loan performance by our underwriting of borrowers and we always hope that no borrower ever misses a payment. Unfortunately life events happen that catch the borrower by surprise and are out of anyone's control, such as a sudden death, divorce, or loss of job. The best advice I can give on protecting your capital invested is to always make sure the collateral is worth at least 30%-40% more than the invested capital or loan. Even with this advice, there is risk of loss for some of the capital. We will discuss in later chapters how to manage all the risks associated with mortgage lending.

Protection of capital investment advice

One answer to the risk management question is to not lend more than 60-65% of the value of the asset. There will be more answers throughout the book.

Key question #9: Is the mortgage loan providing a benefit to the borrower?

It is crucial when being a successful private lender for each loan to provide a clear benefit to the borrower. Often, the lender only focuses on risk management or the rate of return and does not pay enough attention to "how the loan will help the borrower." If the borrower does not have a very clear benefit that drove him or her to borrow the money, the lender runs a risk that the borrower will not perform under the loan terms. Most people have heard about the pleasure/pain theory or the concept where people move toward pleasure and away from pain. I like to ask: *"Is the loan causing pain or giving pleasure to the borrower?"* I have rarely witnessed a borrower walk away from the obligation when they have enough pain associated with defaulting on the loan or when they gain something by keeping the loan and the property. The key to all loan structures is to make sure all borrowers have something big to lose or gain within the loan transaction. What do I mean? If there is enough of the borrower's capital or equity in the property, they will have a lot to lose if they lose the property to foreclosure. Conversely if there is enough equity in the property or if the borrower sells the property where they are protecting this cash they are less likely to default.

In 2008, borrowers walked away in record numbers from their loan obligations because of two very important reasons: they had very little capital invested and they had nothing to gain or protect by keeping the property. This is a disaster waiting to happen. There is clear evidence that when borrowers put down a larger sum of capital down when purchasing a home, they are not likely to walk away from their mortgage obligation.

In addition to the concept describing pleasure or pain there is one other concept that is more important when we discuss the borrower benefit. The borrower's "use of funds" absolutely must help the borrower in some way. Is the loan improving or worsening the borrower's financial situation? If the loan is not improving the borrower's financial situation, then the loan should not be made. A lender who wants to get repaid must provide a solid benefit to the borrower and a smart lender will walk away from a loan that does not show arguable evidence of borrower benefit.

Borrower benefit advice

Never invest in a mortgage loan or provide financing to a borrower who is not benefiting from the use of your money.

<u>Key question #10</u>: What are the mortgage loan amount minimums and maximums?

Mortgage lenders typically set the minimum and maximum loan amounts they will consider and most lenders will establish a targeted average loan amount. This is an important factor to consider for the investors' risk and exposure, especially when investing in a pool of mortgages or a loan fund. For example, a loan portfolio totaling $20,000,000 that is made up of loans averaging $200,000 is far different than one that averages $10,000,000.

Several good questions investors should consider are:

1. How many loans make up the loan pools or fund?
2. What is the highest amount of exposure on any one loan?
3. What percentage of assets is invested in any particular size of loan or loans?
4. Are any loans substantially over the maximum within the guidelines?

I became aware of a fund that invested in 11 loans totaling 62 million dollars or an average of 5.6 million each. This loan pool or fund was funded by approximately 300 investors for an average investment of 200k each. From what I could tell the average loan to value on these loans were 90%. I said to myself that if one of these loans went into default these investors would risk losing principal. Sure enough, a year later I was offered to buy these loans from this fund at 50% of the face amount of principle because ALL of the loans went into default. My understanding is the investors lost a good portion of their original investment. The point of this story is that an investor has to look at the loan size and the percentage of each loan in the entire fund or loan pool to ensure that a concentration of risk does not exist where one or two loans could have a material impact on the overall loan pool or fund performance.

Loan size advice

If you are new to mortgage investing start out small. If you are investing in loan pools or a loan fund, know the loan size parameters of the fund before investing and make sure the fund is not exposed to an excessively high concentration of risk from any one loan.

Key question #11: Does the mortgage loan comply with all laws?

Needless to say, every bank, non-bank, and private lender should comply with all local, state and federal laws surrounding the lending of money. We will briefly discuss later in this book the specific lending laws that a private investor or lender should understand. The good news is that as a private investor who is only lending for commercial properties or business purposes, the laws for mortgage loans in most states are favorable. All private investors investing in mortgage loans should have a good real estate lawyer representing them, to ensure compliance with proper documentation and proper lending practices. Proper loan documentation is an obvious requirement when becoming a private lender, as each state may have a specific requirement when preparing loan closing documents. I often teach entrepreneurs about having a solid mastermind group. A mastermind group is a group of experts that all business people need around them to succeed. I will cover the mastermind group or team in later chapters.

The mastermind group that I suggest to all mortgage investors to create is composed of the following:

o   Real Estate Lawyer
o   Insurance broker

o   Title Company
o   Realtor
o   Contractor

Lending laws and loan compliance advice

My best advice is to engage an experienced real estate lawyer. If you are investing in mortgages through a fund or pool make sure the fund has legal representation by an experienced real estate lawyer. If you are going to invest directly as a private lender, locate a lawyer in the state that you plan to originate your loans. There are a ton of lawyers who can guide you to safely originate loans as a private investor and I would start by contacting a local title company for a referral.

Make sure you have your mastermind group lined up if you are going to proceed alone as a private mortgage investor.

In other words

- ❖ Make sure you ONLY make first mortgage loans, no second mortgages.
- ❖ ONLY lend on commercial or non-consumer mortgage loans; no consumer loans.
- ❖ ONLY lend in geographic markets that you are familiar with.
- ❖ Make sure you know the value range and marketability of the loan collateral.
- ❖ Make sure you know the credit profile or character risk of the borrower(s) to properly price the default risk of the loan.
- ❖ Only make short term loans of 5 year or less; preferably 3 years or less.
- ❖ Price the loan according to default and capital risk, but never less than 5% over 10 year treasuries.
- ❖ Structure the loan so that your principal or capital investment is always protected by the real estate collateral upon liquidation.
- ❖ Never provide a mortgage to a borrower that is NOT benefiting from the money you are loaning.
- ❖ All borrowers must feel some level of financial pain if they default, or obtain some level of financial gain from not defaulting.
- ❖ Be cautious of an excessively high concentration of loans to one borrower.

Risk in loan pools or in a fund should be spread out over many loans. The maximum exposure or concentration of risk should be limited to 10-15% of a portfolio.

❖ Include an experienced mortgage lending attorney as part of your mastermind group or team.

❖ Setup your mastermind group if you are going to go it alone as a private mortgage investor.

BE THE BANK:

Chapter 5:
Real Mortgage Transactions to get you excited to Invest

HERE'S WHAT WE COVER IN THIS CHAPTER:

- We will review more background of private mortgage lending
- I provide some interesting lending stories from the past
- We will review actual funded and paid off loans
- We will review a loan pool that has paid off
- Chapter Summary

LET ME FIRST TELL YOU MY STORY

When I tell people about my high returns on some of the mortgage investments, the response I usually get is: "That sounds way too good to be true" or "That borrower must have been desperate, who would pay those interest rates and fees to borrow money?" I would respond the same way every time: "The borrower needed my money to solve a problem or make more money". I mentioned previously in this book that ALL borrowers should benefit from borrowing money from lenders. This is the reason borrowers do agree to pay fees and interest for the use of the money. Everyone I know has borrowed money, but unfortunately the available capital or borrowing sources are not readily available for a percentage of our population.

When I first got into the mortgage loan business it was before I owned my own house. I too, immediately questioned the mindset of the borrowers that needed the high-cost money. I quickly realized that to a large percentage of the borrowing population, the banks were not willing to lend them money. Now my career officially began in 1984, just before the savings and loan crisis went into full swing, so over the past 31 years, many changes have taken place in the banking and mortgage industry and many lenders have come and gone. In many of the years in which I was providing mortgage loans, the local savings and loan would lend to a large percentage of people that are my borrowers today. Today, the regulations after 2008 and the reduced capital the banks have available, have caused them to be afraid and refrain from lending unless there is almost no risk to the transaction; meaning a perfect loan without much risk of any default. It is good that this is the case today, because if it were not for the changing landscape of the banking guidelines, I would not be so excited about writing this book. Banks and all lenders seem to move from too aggressive to too conservative as markets shift. As a lender, it is good to be part of the lending system when the banks are not taking on much risk, as it allows private lenders to lend money to some very good borrowers at good returns. I say to you: "Why should the banks get to make the money lending, but not you?"

In this chapter I wrote about transactions that were memorable to me and might make you scratch your head in amazement and I focus on a handful of real mortgage transactions that were funded in the recent years by companies owned or controlled by me, the author of this book. My name is Ben Lyons and I like to continually point out that this book is not about borrowing money or lending money to consumers who want to purchase the American dream. This book focuses on lending money to investors so that you, as the mortgage lender/investor, and the borrower each create a financial value because of the transaction. I say it again: "Why should the banks be the only category making money as a lender?" So, BE THE BANK.

OK, so what I want you to see in this chapter and how does it relate to you wanting to invest in mortgages, either in pools, a fund, or as your own private lender? Let's list out the key elements of each transaction, so you can take the information you have learned this far from reading the book and identify the "key elements" or "questions" on each loan and determine if there are patterns to the decisions made. Keep in mind, I wrote this book to: get you, the reader, energized and excited about the income and investment opportunities in lending or investing money in mortgages, and to provide the information required to become a private lender or investor in mortgages.

Please note that I have changed the names of some of the borrowers and not provided the exact address, other than the city and state for each transaction. In the first case study, I received permission from the borrower to use his real name and property address.

LOAN STORIES THAT WILL MAKE YOU SCRATCH YOUR HEAD

The Pizza Shop Lady

One day in 1987, I got a call from a woman who said she needed $35,000 by the next day. I responded by saying that was impossible to do a mortgage loan in 24 hours. She went on to explain to me that her son was in jail and that he had a cocaine problem and he needed to go to drug treatment as soon as possible and her business was in trouble and she had 2 days before she would lose the business. I explained that I needed about a week to fund a mortgage for her on her property and she again said that she needed the money within 24-48 hours. She did something very unusual and she said to me "what if I give you $100,000 worth of jewelry to hold for me until we complete the loan on my house?" I said to her that I knew very little about the value of jewelry but bring it up to me and I will have a jeweler friend tell me what it was worth. Within an hour this woman was in my office with a bag of jewelry. The bag included 2 large diamond earrings that looked about 3 carrots each, a huge diamond ring that she stated was 5 Carrots, and a few rings and a bracelet. She explained to me that her husband passed away and she and her son were running the pizza place that her late husband started and her son's drug habit had cost her everything and the pizza place was about to go under, her credit was horrible, and her son was in jail for theft to fund his drug habit. She went on to say that she only needed the money for a few months because she had the house and the business up for sale and I would be paid off as soon as the house or the business sells. I really felt bad for this woman but I had to decide if it made sense to try to help her. There was no way she could get a loan from a bank or finance company given her situation. I explained to her that I would go down the street to a friend that owns a jewelry store and find out what her bag of jewels was worth and be right back. So about 45 minutes later I came back and told the distraught woman in my office that I would agree to lend her $35,000 as a mortgage on her house today but had to hold onto the bag of jewelry until I appraised her house and obtained a title search that showed what she owed on the house. Her house was appraised at $150,000 and she owed about $60,000 and I would be in a 2nd lien position. I agreed to provide this loan to her subject to holding the jewelry until we recorded the mortgage and I continue to hold the earrings and ring until I am paid down to $20,000 or the loan is paid off. I did this because I typically did not make second mortgages but this woman begged and pleaded with me to re-consider lending her the money and I knew if I held the lien on her house and the two pieces of jewelry that I would be safe so I made the loan. In about 6 months the woman sold the business and I was paid in full. While some of the people reading this might say that I take advantage of people, I like to think of it as helping people who cannot get short term money from banks or finance companies. If I did not help her she might have lost her business and her son might have had to stay in jail so from my perspective I provided a great service. It has always been very important to me for the borrowers to feel they have received a great benefit from the use of my money and in this case the borrower made money when the business was sold by utilizing my money for 6 months.

The Man with the Rolex

This story happened around 1993 when I was brokering Private mortgages and also originating government loans. I was referred to this borrower and for this story we will call him Big Paul. Big Paul called me to get a mortgage to buy a new house for he and his wife. I briefly spoke with Big Paul on the phone in my office and he asked me to come to his office to take the loan application and get the required documentation for the loan. When I arrived at his office in Towson Maryland I went up to the reception desk and in front of me was this beautiful woman who was wearing an extremely tight and short skirt with a silk low cut blouse and let's just say she was not flat chested. Now, I was in my early twenties and was mesmerized by the looks of this woman, she was gorgeous and I said to myself, "wow, this guy Big Paul really hired a very attractive woman to greet new clients." The woman asked me to have a seat and someone will come get me to take me to Big Paul's office. So about a minute later, another unbelievable woman opens the door to the reception area and says "are you Ben?" I could hardly speak because this woman was even more gorgeous than the woman at the reception desk. But I managed to sputter out of my mouth that I was Ben and I am here to see Big Paul. As I followed her back through the office I noticed how nice the office was and said to myself, "wow, two of the most attractive women I have ever seen dressed in a very provocative way and this decked out office, I wonder what this guy does for a living?" So I get to this big office with one of the largest desks I have ever seen and behind was a guy that was large. I mean he was about 6 foot 6 and 290 pounds. For those of you that do not know, I am only 5' 7" tall and weigh about 150 pounds so to me this guy was big. That's why I named him Big Paul. Paul asked me to have a seat and the first words out of his mouth was "aren't those young ladies the hottest women you have ever seen?" At that time in my career, I was very much focused on business so I quickly changed the subject and asked him about the house he was buying and details about his finances. He told me that he was under contract for $400,000 on a house near his office and he needed a loan to purchase the home. I did the usual loan application and obtained all his income documentation and returned to my office a few hours later. As it turned out Big Paul had credit and income issues. Not horrible credit or no income but just did not qualify for Fannie Mae financing so I found a local Savings Bank that agreed to provide Big Paul a mortgage if he put down 25% in cash and paid for closing costs. I called Big Paul and explained that I found him a lender that would provide a mortgage to him if he came up with $100,000 plus about $15,000 in closing costs. I explained to him that I was charging a 2.5% loan broker fee as part of the $15,000 of closing costs. He was ok with the loan and all the fees so I order the appraisal and title and we completed the loan process over the next few weeks. A week before closing I confirmed with Big Paul that he needed to bring $115,000 to closing in order to complete the transaction and he stated that would not be a problem. I asked him to provide proof of the money to close and he sent me a statement showing $70,000. I asked him where the rest of the proof of funds were and he told me not to worry about it that he would have it. Because I was just the mortgage broker in this transaction, I had to follow the banks requirements of "proof of funds" to close so I continued to ask Big Paul where the funds to close were coming from and he provided about $102,000 of the $115,000 he needed so the bank allowed the loan to continue on to closing. I repeatedly asked Big Paul for proof of funds to close and he kept telling me not to worry about it so I went along with his wishes and the loan closing was scheduled.

The loan closing, I will never forget

The loan closing for the purchase of this home Big Paul was buying was taking place at 5pm on a Friday night at the real estate brokers office. In attendance at the loan closing were the sellers who were a husband and wife and they spoke no English, the seller's realtor, and the seller's daughter as the translator. For the buyer's side was Big Paul and his wife, and the buyer's realtor. Additionally, the loan closing attorney was conducting the closing for the bank. One of the first actions in a loan closing is the review of the Closing statement or HUD. This shows how much all the charges are, how much the seller will get and how much the buyer needs to close. As indicated to Big Paul for 3 weeks, he need approximately $115,000 in certified funds to close. I asked Big Paul to go into another room to discuss it where I explained to him that I could not allow the purchase to take place without getting paid the broker fee. He started to get pissed at me and keep in mind he is 1 foot taller than me and 140 pounds heavier than me so this guy could have killed me pretty easily. He said to me he would have the money within a few days and for me to allow the transaction to close. I said no.

Well, Big Paul begins to explain that he only has $108,000 and that he would have to go to the bank to get the rest. We got up from the table and walked next door to his bank and I waited outside for him. He came outside to say he could not get any money. He then offered up his car title to his brand new corvette that was parked out front of the real estate office. I said, sure, I can hold on to the car title until you come up with the broker fee. He handed me to car registration and the car was not even in his name but titled to someone I never heard of and it had a large lien on it so that did not help him. I went on to say to him that I earned the broker fee and the loan could not close unless I was paid. I worked two months on the loan and he tells me he does not have the money to close until we are all sitting at closing. That was not fair to me or all the people sitting at the closing table. Big Paul corners me up against the wall and gets in my face and he looked like he was going to kill me and says "what the F_ _ _ do you want me to do? You want to hold my watch?" he replied. I looked down at his wrist and saw this incredible Rolex watch. Admittedly, I knew nothing about Rolex watches but I could tell this one had to be worth the seven thousand he owed me. This watch was all gold, had diamonds all around the bezel, and just looked expensive. Big Paul proceeded to take the watch off his wrist and handed it to me. At 7 pm that evening we concluded the closing of his new home. Before I left the closing table, I typed up an agreement that allowed Big Paul one week to bring me the seven thousand dollars he owed me or I was going to keep the watch. Now keep in mind that I was in my early twenties and a fancy watch was not my style. A week went by and Big Paul never called me so I called him and when I got him on the phone he told me to keep the watch then hung up. I called my attorney and asked him if I was legally allowed to keep the watch and he stated yes but I went on to tell him that I did not want the watch as I wanted the seven thousand I was owed. My attorney gave me the phone number and address of a relative of his, that happened to own a pawn shop so I went to downtown Baltimore and delivered the watch to the Pawn broker in exchange for the seven thousand. The Pawn broker first had to run the serial numbers to confirm the watch was not stolen and it came back as not stolen or that the info did not appear to be stolen.

This is not the end of this story.
About 4 weeks go by and I get a phone call from my attorney telling me that the watch I sold to the Pawn shop was purchased at a prominent high end jewelry store a few months ago by Big Paul for twenty-two thousand dollars. He went on to say that Big Paul still owed the jewelry store twenty-one thousand dollars and that the store had just reported it as stolen by Big Paul for non-payment.

Oh wait, this story gets better
About one year later I get another phone call from my friend at the bank that funded the loan to big Paul for his purchase of the home. My friend went on tell me to check the local newspaper for the article on Big Paul. Apparently Big Paul was operating an insurance agency for high profile athletes and business people and instead of using the insurance premiums for the policies he stole the money for personal use. Something in the amount of five hundred thousand dollars. Makes me wonder how much of the down payment for the new house was stolen.

The annuity loan
One of my most profitable loans was somewhat of a sad story about a man who was the only child who inherited his father's estate which consisted of

almost one thousand acres of land and a once successful business. Some-where around 1997 I got a call from a borrower who was referred to me for a mortgage loan. He tried to get a loan from the local bank close to where his family lived and operated as a very successful business for sev-enty-five years. The problem was that the parents and grand-parents had died about eight years ago and the man that called me went on to say that he had no money left from the inheritance and the business was not oper-ating anymore so the banks would not lend him any money. The man on the phone continued to tell me that he had not really ever worked in his life because his parents were wealthy and he was the only child so they gave him everything. I asked him how old he was and he stated he was 39 years old. I thought to myself "never worked before, wow?". The guy needed money to live and he stated that he was trying to get the family business back operating and needed to borrower money. I asked him the usual ques-tions about the collateral, his credit and income and I came to the conclu-sion this guy had millions of dollars of real estate but no money or real income to repay the loan. I told him that I could help him if he agreed to sell the property or prove that he had an income to repay the loan within six months. I drove about an hour to see his properties the next day and I determined that this guy was probably one of the largest land owners in the area and that he had plenty of collateral to get the loan from me. I went on to lend him a few hundred thousand dollars and I held out 12 months of interest payments because he could not afford to make them each month. I strongly suggested to this guy that he put all his real estate up for sale and take the few million dollars he would get and invest it until he finds a way to make a living. He responded like he genuinely appreciated the ad-vice and we left it at that. About four months later he called me again ask-ing for more money. I asked him what happened to the two hundred thousand he borrowed 4 months ago and he stated that he purchased equip-ment for the business and was getting things in order to get the business going but needed more money. So I lent him another two hundred thou-sand dollars. Six months later he calls again and I lent him another two hundred thousand dollars and this went on two more times until he owed me over 1 million dollars. Finally, on the sixth request in less than 2 years I told him that he needed to sell his property and get me paid off because I was not lending him anymore money. I actually had to file a foreclosure action against him to force him to realize he needed to do something. I told him he could deed me the property and I will sell it for him and we can split the profits but he ended up selling the property to a local developer and walked with about five hundred thousand dollars and I am sure he squandered that money away in a matter of a year. As much as I had tried to counsel this guy and show him how he could turn his real estate into cash so that he could lend it out he just wanted the immediate cash in hand and in the end made the wrong decisions. If he sold the property immediately and walked with 1.5 million in cash and loaned it out at 10% annually, he would have an annual income of $150,000 without touching his asset account.

My first foreclosure – the Drugstore in Cumberland Maryland

In 1987 I was only 21 years old at the time but had already been in the Mortgage, Real estate and Private lending business for three years. Until this time, I had not had to foreclose on anyone or been responsible for a foreclosure so I learned a good lesson on my first one. Perhaps this foreclosure gave me a false sense of security or strong belief in lending money but nonetheless this story illustrates how interesting the private lending business can be or perhaps how foolish I was at such a young age.

One of my traits after about a year in the business was that I would guarantee the investors that invested money with me that they would not lose principle capital because I was so sure of myself. Looking back, this was very naive of me because I did not know from experience about market corrections or that I would go on to produce 5 billion dollars in mortgage loans. Guaranteeing a few million did not seem reckless but I certainly would not guarantee hundreds of millions or billions to investors. But, at a very young age I learned how to make a lot of money and my ego was extremely high. At age 20, I made more money than both my parents did combined and my dad had a master's degree in computer science and I did not go to college so I thought I was the cat's meow.

One day, I get a call from the president of Regal Bank, a local savings Bank, where the Bank president and a few friends provided capital for the private loans I was making. The bank president went on to tell me to get ready for my guarantee because one of the loans was in default and the foreclosure auction was set for two weeks from now. Even though I was earning good money at the time I had a sinking feeling in my stomach. I said to myself that I do not have the money to pay off that mortgage to the investor. I hung up the phone and looked into the loan file for details on when the loan was made and other information about the loan. The property was a beat up, very old residential property but appeared to have enough value to return the original principle to the investor. The day of the auction I get a call from the bank president saying to me "Hey Ben, congratulations, you own a new property in Cumberland Maryland and what name do you want to buy it in?". He went on to tell me that the payoff to him was $78,214.87. I said, "wait a minute, the principle balance was only $65,000, why do you say I owe you over 78 thousand?" He explained to me that the property taxes for 2 years had to be paid, fire insurance, legal and foreclosure expenses and finally auctioneer expenses totaling the seventy-eight thousand was due. So now I really had a sick to my stomach feeling and thought I was going to throw up. Seventy-eight thousand dollars in 1987 was a lot of money and who knows how much more in repairs and other expenses I had to pay. Keep in mind I am 20 years old and this was my first foreclosure.

The next day, I called a local realtor from the yellow pages (no internet then) and the realtor said he would meet me at the property later that week. On the Friday of that week I meet the local realtor in this moderately priced city community suburb of Cumberland Maryland. The realtor said his initial reaction is the property would sell for about $70,000 because of the poor condition it was in and I was thinking oh shit, that means I need to come up with around fifteen thousand to make the investors whole after real estate commissions. The realtor said to me that he wanted to do a market analysis and also look into the zoning of the property. I drove the three hours back home and was really upset and worried the entire ride back. The next day I get a phone call from the realtor asking me how much I needed to be paid off in full and that he thought the property had commercial zoning which would allow me to sell for more. I stated seventy-eight thousand dollars and he said ok and hung up the phone. On Sunday, which was the following day I get a call from the same realtor saying he had the property sold and I would clear eighty thousand dollars. I could not believe my ears and was so happy and hung up without asking any other questions.

A few weeks later, I was asked to come back to Cumberland Maryland for a loan closing where I would sell this property and collect the check for my investor and pocket about $1,800. I show up to the closing and the buyer is in the room with me. After we signed all the papers and I get my checks I asked the buyer who he was and he went on to tell me that he represented the drugstore chain on the corner across the street that they wanted my corner because it was larger footprint than the one they were in now. I asked a question to this guy that will stick with me forever. I said "I am just curious; how much more would you have paid for this corner?" The extremely nice man went on to tell me probably as high as fifty thousand more than the purchase price. I left the closing and drove back thinking that I could have just made fifty thousand dollars more had I taken the time to get educated on what I truly had. Had I recognized that the business properties that were on the remaining 3 corners of the intersection where my collateral was and that I owned the only one used as residential I would have understood the commercial value versus the residential value I would have fifty more dollars in my pocket. While I should have been pleased that I got paid in full very quickly from the foreclosure I learned an invaluable lesson that day.

The furniture guy going to Belgium

The year was 1985 and I was sitting in my office on a Friday afternoon around two thirty getting ready to leave for the day when the phone rings. I had paid to have a small ad in the money to loan section of the Baltimore Sun and someone was calling from that ad. I answered the phone as I always did at that time by saying, "Thanks for calling, my name is Ben Lyons and how can I be of service to you?" The caller was a man with a deep voice and the first words out of his mouth was "do you believe you can complete a loan for me secured by my property within twenty-four hours?" I responded, "it depends on many factors." He quickly interrupted and said, my question is "do you believe you can complete a loan for me within twenty-four hours?" So I said, "yes, I do believe I can complete a loan for you within twenty-four hours."

He then went on to explain to me his situation that he was leaving for Belgium on Sunday and needed to borrower $40,000 to take with him to Belgium in order to purchase certain rights to sell furniture manufactured in the United States. I quickly went into focus mode and began asking questions. I had to immediately find out if the real estate value of his property will support the loan and the we needed to get title completed right away. Keep in mind this is 1985, we did not have Google, Zillow, or anything that resembled the tools of today. After the application was taken and the information was obtained I told him we needed the payoff on his first mortgage in writing and I needed to have someone go to the courthouse within the next two hours and get a title abstract completed on his property. We agreed to speak within the next hour. At this time, it was three thirty on Friday afternoon and I had about an hour and half to complete this guy's loan file. I called my go-to private lender and the local Bank President, Stewart and told him about the deal and I asked him if he thought he could get the funds by the next day if this deal was good. He said yes, so I immediately called his wife Betsy who was a title abstractor and asked her to run down to the courthouse and pull the abstract before 6pm when they closed. By 6pm we had the title search completed on the borrowers house and I had the payoff on his first mortgage in hand. The only thing left to do was to see the collateral which we scheduled a site visit for Saturday morning. Additionally, if the site visit went well we had to complete the loan closing documents. The next morning at 8am I picked up Stewart from his very large house and drove him to Columbia Maryland where we walked through the borrower's house and drove around the neighborhood to deter- mine the value of the collateral. We concluded that his house was valued at around $210,000 and we were loaning him a total of $130,000. He had to pay off his first mortgage and he needed to walk with $35,000 to take with him to Belgium. We charged this borrower 18% and 8 points on this loan but the borrower was extremely grateful. The story is not over because at 2pm on Sat- urday, or less than twenty-four hours from his initial call to me, we closed on the guy's loan and we handed him a check for $35,000. He took the check and said, wait, I cannot do anything with this check in Belgium, I need cash! Stew- art and I looked at him and said, "what?" The best part about this deal is that Stewarts brother in law owned a liquor store and he had $35,000 in cash avail- able to cash this check for this borrower and so the borrower left for Belgium the next day with his cash in hand and he called me a Hero. He said to me on Saturday afternoon that he called over twenty companies and asked the ques- tion "do you believe you can get a loan closed in twenty-four hours?" and I was the ONLY one that said yes to him. Truth be told, I really did not believe I could get it completed in twenty-four hours but it goes to show you that you can do a lot when you believe you can and set your mind to it.

MY FAVORITE CASE STUDY: # 1: CENTRAL AVENUE DEAL

Deal Background: Jeff Thomas was referred to me by a mortgage broker that Jeff had been working with to refinance his mortgage on his retail shopping center that he owned in Waldorf Maryland. Jeff called me up to tell me his story. It went like this.

"Hello Ben, I hope you can help me! I need a loan to pay off my 1st mortgage with PNC Bank."

"OK what is the situation?" I replied.

Jeff went on to tell me that the bank wanted him to pay down his mortgage that had a principal balance at that time of $979,791 by more than 400k in cash or payoff the loan in full within 90 days. It was July 2009 when Jeff went on to tell me he had received a call and a letter telling him he had 90 days to pay the loan down or off or the bank was going to foreclose. Jeff pleaded with the bank but they would not budge from their position. Now, keep in mind that Jeff was current on his mortgage payments at the time, but the bank felt it needed to lower its exposure or something similar and was requiring Jeff to find a solution to the problem for the bank. The bank's problem became Jeff's problem. Jeff called his attorney and explained what the bank wanted from him. It was my understanding that Jeff's attorney suggested Jeff to immediately stop making the monthly mortgage payments. The theory behind this advice was that because Jeff was current on his loan it could not go through the "workout" department. Only defaulted loans could be addressed through this department. So, at the advice of his attorney, Jeff stopped paying the mortgage to the bank. While this seems strange, it is a common theme from 2008 to 2011. At this point, Jeff joins the ranks of a "deadbeat borrower" or one that is a bad credit risk in the eyes of the banking system as a result of the defaulted mortgage.

Before we go on to the transaction let me describe the property. See in the photo below the actual property.

- Property description: Office and Retail Property
- *Building Size: 12,500 SF*
- *Building Class: C*
- *Lot Size: 1.40 AC*
- *10 separate leasable units*
- *Gross rents at time of loan application was $131,400 per year*
- *Potential gross rents were $163,200 if fully leased*
- *Estimated annual expenses were $36,000*
- *Current net income was approximately $95,000 annually*

Now for the good part, Jeff believed through discussion with the workout department of the bank that the bank would accept a discount to the remaining payoff, if they could remove the loan from their books quickly. Keep in mind that from what I could tell, the building had enough net cash flow to cover the monthly mortgage payment to the bank. Nonetheless, the bank wanted the loan off their books. In my normal course of doing business I always go look at the property that is being utilized as collateral to see for myself what it is worth and what I believe would happen if I foreclosed or had to liquidate the property rather quickly. When I went to see the property and do my walk through the first thing I noticed was the "For Sale" sign on the property. I asked Jeff and he confirmed that the property was for sale. So I wrote down the realtor's name and phone number from the sign and continued my visit. When I returned to the office, I called the listing agent and I then learned it was listed for sale for $1.25 million. Just wait, it gets better… The realtor went on to say that the doctor who owns the building next door may be putting in an offer to buy the building.

OK, you may be thinking ahead and can predict what happened next. Before I tell you, let's organize and enumerate the facts so far.

- The current owner was Jeff Thomas
- Jeff purchased the building in 2000 for $860,000
- Jeff borrowed $975,000 from PNC sometime after the purchase
- The building generated $95,000 in net income in 2009 when I got involved
- The potential net income was $127,000 if fully leased
- Jeff had pretty good credit until he defaulted on loan, when bank demanded a pay down of principal.
- Property was listed for sale for $1,250,000 when I visited the property

So, what was our plan? We contacted his current mortgage holder and got them to agree to a payoff of $575,000 if we paid them off within 30 days. We then provided Jeff a new first mortgage of $650,000 with fees of 6%, an interest rate of 18% annually and a 6% additional fee at the time the loan was paid off. This is called an exit fee. So, on an annual basis we charged Jeff 30% for the use of the money. I know, you are saying to yourself that this guy is a crook and Jeff is an idiot. Now, let's go on with the rest of the story before you jump to conclusions.

If you spoke with Jeff today, he would tell you I am the greatest thing since sliced bread. His exact quote was: "You made me more money than anyone I know." The math is simple, he owed the bank at the time of payoff $1,075,000 and we were able to get them to accept $575,000 but with all our fees it came to $650,000. Basically, we made him $425,000 plus the additional equity from the sale of the building. From the date we closed to him putting the funds in his pocket it took exactly 6 months to the day because he had a contract from the doctor next door to purchase Jeff's building for $1.2 million. The cost of our money was irrelevant if Jeff could use it to benefit him at this amount.

So let's break down this deal from a risk perspective

New loan was $650,000 or probably 55% of retail value (high range of value) and 80% of quick sale value. So I figured based on the income approach, cost approach, and market approach to value the property was worth between $1.1 million on the high end and 800k under forced sale conditions or low end. If I got stuck with the loan and was owed $700,000 and the property generated $95,000 in net income, my return on the $700,000 would be 13.57%. This assumed that the income stayed the same at $95,000.

But, here was the best part. From speaking with the commercial realtor who had the building listed for sale at $1,250,000, I asked him if I could speak with the potential buyer. If you remember I stated that there was a doctor who had his office next door and he owned the building he was in, but was possibly interested in purchasing Jeff's property. Without going into great detail and to sum it up, I convinced Jeff to take the $1.1 million offer from the doctor and after exactly 6 months, Jeff sold his building and put 500k in his pocket, of which 425k was because of the availability of private funding. Now, let's break down who got what:

- The buyer (the doctor) wins because he felt he got a good deal at 1.1 million.
- The seller (Jeff) walked away with over $500,000, of which $425,000 was because the mortgage he had with the bank was sold at a deep discount. He would have likely received less than 50k had he paid off the $975,000 loan that had a likely payoff of over 1 million. Jeff pocketed over $375,000 more after all was said and done because of this transaction.
- I earned a 6% origination fee of $39,000 plus 24% interest on $650,000 for 6 months or $78,000 for a total income on this one deal of $117,000 or 36% interest based on an annual return.
- PNC bank might think they did well because they got the loan off their books fast.
- In this deal, everyone appears to win.

Ok, so why after tens of thousands of loan transactions is this my favorite deal? When you have a borrower like Jeff who is so very appreciative of your skills of making him $375,000 that he would not otherwise have made and along the way we profit at a 36% annual rate on our capital, I call that a victory for all parties involved. Jeff was so impressed with what we had done for him that he ended up becoming a private mortgage investor and invested $250,000 of his proceeds with me in other mortgage loan transactions.

CASE STUDY # 2: WOODCREST HOLDINGS

My phone rang at about 9 am on a Tuesday morning.

"Ben Lyons, good morning!" I answered in the usual way.

"Hello Ben, are you lending private money these days?" the voice asked.

"Well, depends on how good the deal is and by the way, who is on the phone?" I responded. Actually, I should have instantly figured it out because the voice on the other end was a voice from my past.

"It's Roman, and this deal is right up your alley." So Roman went on to describe the deal. Once he got to the part about the loan being 5 million dollars I said:

"Hold up," I don't have 5 million dollars available right now." Somehow Roman did not want to hear me that I did not have the amount of money needed and he kept on explaining the loan transaction. Not only did Roman say the loan request was 5 million but he went on to say:

"Oh, and the guy needs the money in 3 weeks."

"I can't close a 5 million dollar loans in less than 3 weeks!" I said laughing at the idea.

"Ben," he said, "I know you and I know you would love this deal". Somehow Roman was so convincing that I said to email me the details of the loan request. The deal details were as follows:

- Blaco construction obtained the winning bid at auction for 4.3 million of a partially developed 94-unit townhouse project in Washington DC
- Blaco put down $900,000 deposit at the auction and if they did not close on the transaction within 3 weeks, the deposit would be forfeited
- Blaco needed a loan of 3 million to close on the purchase and another 2 million to complete the 26 townhomes that were 90% completed.
- The collateral for the loan was the entire 94 unit project, of which 26 townhomes were partially completed and the remaining project was fully approved and ready for building permit.
- Blaco had a total of 1.5 million in cash to use to purchase.
- Blaco construction was owned by Roger Black. Roger and his wife also owned a title company that generated about $700,000 in net income per year.
- Borrower thought the estimated "as is" value was over 10 million.
- I visited the property and estimated it to be worth 8-9 million at the time.
- We obtained an appraisal valuing the property at 12 million.

So back to the story…. With the information provided to me via email, Roman appeared to be accurate in saying that I would love the deal. The next day I flew from the Orlando office to Washington DC to visit the property. It was a very hot summer day when I met the borrower at the property. I spent about 1 hour walking the site and interviewing the borrower and about 1 hour driving around the neighborhood. The borrower explained that he had two and a half weeks to close or he was going to lose his $900,000 deposit, so he wanted assurance that I could close the deal in time. I explained that I needed to complete the file review and would get back with him in a day or two. So with that statement to the borrower, the borrower told me he would have to continue to look elsewhere for a loan commitment. During the next two days I reviewed the marketplace and confirmed the value range of the Townhouse units and the estimated cost to complete the phase 1 of the project. With my evaluation and meeting with my credit committee, Company President at that time Marc Caramuta, our CFO Matt brothers and largest investor and Director Alex Fink, we concluded to approve the deal. The challenge for us is that we had 2 weeks to close on this transaction or the buyer loses $900,000 deposit. The deal I had approved was structured as follows:

- 5.5 million dollars 1st mortgage
- 13% interest only for 12 months
- 2 million in escrow to complete phase 1 or 26 townhouses & condos.
- Initial advance at closing 3.3 million, borrower bringing 1 million down payment plus all closing costs for a total cash outlay of 1.5 million
- Payment reserves covering 12 months of payments collected at closing
- Copy of previously completed phase 1 environmental report
- Obtain an appraisal of 10 million or higher
- Personal and corporate guarantees
- 3 points to us as lender

We quickly scrambled to obtain an appraisal, even though we were more than fine closing the transaction prior to receiving it, because we were very confident that phase 1, which consisted of 26 residences that were 95% completed, would likely sell for an average price of $300,000 putting just phase 1 value at over 7.5 million. The property appraised for 10 million "as is" and 12 million "subject to completion of phase 1" so we closed the transaction just before the borrower's deadline and within the 2 weeks. The loan closed on March 6, 2014 and paid off on September 1, 2015. Our fund generated approximately $940,000 in revenue in 18 months or approximately a 14.5% annual return.

Let me share with you an interesting twist to this story because of the significant impact it had on me during a 24-hour period and also a life lesson about "determination under pressure." So, I mentioned in previous paragraphs that I had 2.5 weeks to raise 3.3 million, which was the amount of capital my company had to advance at closing on or before March 6, 2014. Two weeks earlier than March 6th, I gave Roger Black, the buyer, the promise that our company would fund his purchase. He called me every day to make sure we were funding his loan, as he reminded me every call that if we did not fund as scheduled, he would lose his deposit of $900,000. Since LYNK Capital at the time was funding other transactions, it did not have all of the 3.3 million needed to fund the loan and as a result had been in dialogue with a source of funds that verbally agreed to put up half of the 3.3 million if LYNK put up the remaining half. With this knowledge and believed assurances that all 3.3 million was available to fund the purchase, I proceeded to work on completing the loan file and preparing for loan closing. I will never forget the call I received at 8:47 PM on March 5th from Tim Spolar, of Alliance Partners with his boss Joe Kenary. The call went like this:

"Ben, listen, we are not funding the 2.5 million of this deal because we are not comfortable with you."

"What the hell are you talking about, not comfortable with me?" I responded.

"We found an issue on your background from 12 years ago where you had defaulted on a 2.3-million-dollar loan from Susquehanna bank," this guy Joe went on to say.

"That is ridiculous, the loan was paid 11 years ago and I am not the borrower on this project you guys have agreed to participate in." I went on to explain the seemingly defaulted loan was a construction loan that ballooned and was paid within 60 days of the default 11 years ago. "Why would you guys care about an issue 12 years ago? Furthermore, your company is investing in Roger Blacks project at Blaco construction, not me," I continued.

Anyway, without hesitation, this guy Joe, who knew nothing about me, at 9 pm on the night before my company needed 3.3 million to fund Rogers loan, backed out of the deal and there was nothing I could say to convince this guy that he was making an inaccurate assessment of me and a poor business decision and likely causing the contract purchaser to lose $900,000 he put down as a deposit at the auction. For those who don't know much about me, when I give someone my word, I honor it, so with that I knew I could not let Blaco construction down and needed to raise 2 million dollars by 5pm the next day. Yes, you read this correctly, in order for our company to honor the funding for our borrower I need to raise 2 million dollars before 5pm on March 6th. To cut right to the chase, I did raise the money and owe many thanks to my good friends and business partners like Alex Fink who provided 1 million and Paul Bekman, Jay Dackman, and John Schmitz who provided the other million just by me asking and explaining the deal. It felt good to deliver the funds to finance the mortgage for Roger Black of Blaco and as they say, "the rest is history." LYNK Capital went on to make over 1 million dollars including the points, fees and interest income and Blaco construction is projected to make a 5-7 million dollars profit.

Blaco construction sold the first 26 units of the project or phase 1 for approximately 9 million dollars and paid the LYNK Capital fund back in 15 months.
So on phase 1 alone, the borrower was able to net over 2 million dollars and
still have the remaining project to sell. An aerial view of project at time of closing is below.

CASE STUDY # 3 – 41ST STREET DEAL

Balaram Owens came to me from a well-established mortgage broker. The
mortgage broker previously was part of my loan team and knew exactly how
to review loans for me to fund them. I illustrate this case study because the
loan that was funded and ultimately paid off represents a core business that
exists as a result of the real estate collapse of 2008 and changes in our banking
system and regulatory environment. What was once a core loan product for
community banks has gone away after the 2008 financial crisis and this void
allowed many private lenders like myself to make excellent risk adjusted returns. So let me outline this transaction below.

Buyer is a real estate broker and an investor. He purchased a bank-owned va-
cant property in May, 2010 for $65,000. He brought $16,000 plus his original
deposit in cash to closing and also pledged a condo owned free and clear as

additional collateral. I required the additional collateral so that my loan to value requirements were met. If you recall from previous chapters, this is called a blanket loan. I lent him $127,000 for 12 months at 14% interest. The loan included me holding a repair escrow for $60,390 to complete the renovation and also I charged 4 origination points and the broker charged 4 points. Yes, this was a very expensive loan for this borrower. I believe originally, Balaram was going to resell the house for immediate profits but he decided to rent the property once it was renovated. According to Balaram, he received rental income of $1,650 per month. My loan was for 1 year, however I agreed to extend the loan term for another 2 years because Balaram always paid his mortgage payment on time. Besides, I was earning 14% on my investment and the real estate values in Washington DC were increasing year over year in 2010 through 2012. My understanding from speaking with Balaram is that he sold the property on December 13, 2013 for $260,000. Based on the costs to sell and the negative carry costs during the rental period, Balaram made approximately $100,000 net profit from the sale after paying me 14% interest and fees for 3.5 years. I earned $62,230 in interest income plus the $6,000 in points and fees when we closed, so I earned $68,230 in total income in 3.5 years on this one loan.

I am sure you are still raising the same objection when you are reading this: "Why in the world would Balaram pay this high of an interest rate?" I am sure Balaram went to his local lender or bank and they said no and he wanted to close on this money-making opportunity, so he justified the return he was paying to me by recognizing how much he could make for himself. I often get asked about the "ridiculous" interest rate I charge borrowers for lending them the money and I like to tell these stories about how the use of my money has benefited thousands of borrowers who are locked out of the banking system and unable to obtain capital to execute on their business. If Balaram made $100,000 by using some of his money and mostly my money, then he has made a smart decision versus not doing the transaction at all. I am certain if banks and other non-bank lenders made it easier to borrower cheaper money than that is where he would have gone. It is no different than Balaram and I becoming business partners in the deal.

CASE STUDY # 4 – MY LOAN PORTFOLIO FROM 2009 -2011

The report below represents a list of funded loans by me from 2009 to 2011 and illustrates some key indicators of what a mortgage pool could represent. Please note that this portfolio was funded as a "part time" business of mine and not a full time strategy but is a very good illustration of very high yielding ways to invest your money in private mortgages.

Lyons Private mortgage portfolio											
Borrower	Property Type	LTV	Original Note Date	Original Note Amount	Original Note Rate	Original Points and Non 3rd Party	Original Maturity Date	Date Repaid	Performed According to Terms	loss from sale	Holding time (yrs)
Libowitz	SFD	22%	4/30/09	$290,000	9.75%	2.75%; $595 Admin Fee	5/1/2010	1/18/2011	Yes		1.72
Truesdale	SFD	60%	6/4/09	$109,200	15%	5% points; 3 Inspection	7/1/2010	6/19/2014	Yes		5.04
Immovable City LLC	SFD	63%	7/15/09	$158,000	14%	4%; $350 Admin; $300 Inspection Fees	8/1/2010	2/1/2010	Yes		0.55
Jovetic	THS	49%	8/14/09	$115,000	14%	4% points $495 Admin $300 Inspection	9/1/2010	1/15/2015	No	0	5.00
Thomas	Business Center	60%	11/16/09	$650,000	24%	6% points	11/16/2010	5/7/2010	Yes		0.47
Brodie/Owens	Condo	37%	1/14/10	$56,000	14%	4%; $495 Admin Fee	2/1/2011	7/12/2010	Yes		0.49
Joy	SFD	65%	2/16/10	$144,000	12%	4%; $495 Admin Fee; $150 Inspection Fee	2/1/2011	6/11/2010	Yes		0.32
Galvin	SFD	65%	2/19/10	$141,700	13%	3%; $495 Admin Fee	3/1/2011	8/20/2010	Yes		0.50
Hooks	SFD	42%	2/26/10	$107,000	14%	3%; $295 Admin Fee	3/1/2011	9/7/2011	Yes		1.53
Hooks	SFD	36%	2/26/10	$95,000	14%	5%; $495 Admin Fee	3/1/2011	10/21/2013	No	-25,687	3.65
Joy	SFD	64%	3/15/10	$140,000	13%	3%; $495 Admin Fee	4/1/2011	9/23/2010	Yes		0.53
McClosky	SFD	35%	3/25/10	$175,000	13%	2.5%; $495 Admin Fee	4/1/2011	2/15/2013	No	-5,265	2.90
Stephens	SFD	52%	4/8/10	$195,000	13%	5%; $495 Admin Fee	5/1/2011	3/21/2011	Yes		0.95
Jennings	SFD	62%	4/29/10	$142,000	13%	5%; $495 Admin; $450 Inspection Fee	5/1/2011	3/18/2011	Yes		0.88
McClosky	SFD	75%	5/14/10	$260,000	15%	5%; $495 Admin Fee	6/1/2011	9/20/2011	No	0	1.35
Joy	SFD	65%	5/17/10	$152,500	13%	5%; $495 Admin Fee	6/1/2011	10/27/2010	Yes		0.45
Brodie/Owens	THS	55%	5/28/10	$127,000	14%	8%; $495 Admin Fee	6/1/2011	12/23/2013	Yes		3.58

Woodruff	SFD	60%	6/4/10	132,000	16%	6%; $495 Admin; $450 Inspection Fees	7/1/2011	10/20/2010	Yes		0.38
Davis	SFD	48%	6/18/10	$130,000	16%	6%; $495 Admin Fee; $450 Inspection Fee	7/1/2011	12/17/2010	Yes		0.50
Sanderlin	SFD	58%	6/25/10	$118,000	15%	6%; $450 Inspection Fees	7/1/2011	9/14/2011	Yes		1.22
Sykes	4 UNIT	56%	6/28/10	$150,000	15%	6%; $495 Admin Fee; $600 Inspection Fee	7/1/2011	8/3/2011	Yes		1.10
Herzenberg	SFD	50%	6/29/10	$600,000	13%	5%; $495 Admin;	7/1/2011	9/2/2011	Yes		1.18
Labanowski	5 UNIT	47%	7/9/10	$150,000	16%	6%; $495 Admin	7/1/2011	7/2/2012	Yes		1.98
Collins	CONDO	59%	7/15/10	$65,000	15%	6%; $495 Admin Fee; $700 Inspection Fee	8/1/2011	9/30/2010	Yes		0.21
Yi	SFD	42%	7/16/10	$242,500	13%	5.5%; $495 Admin; inspection fees $600	8/1/2011	12/1/2011	Yes		1.38
Yi	SFD	65%	7/30/10	$120,250	13%	5%; $495 Admin; $600 Inspection Fees	8/1/2011	3/23/2012	Yes		1.65
Cummings	SFD	41%	8/12/10	$76,000	15%	6%; $495 Admin Fee; $600 Inspection Fee	9/1/2011	8/3/2011	Yes		0.98
Atkins	SFD	42%	8/24/10	$175,000	13%	5%; $495 Admin; $900 Inspection Fees	9/1/2011	6/3/2011	Yes		0.78
Pham	SFD	50%	9/14/10	$98,000	16%	7%; $495 Admin; $750 Inspection fees	10/1/2011	2/28/2011	Yes		0.46
Finkelstein	THS	65%	9/17/10	$201,500	13%	5%; $495 Admin	10/1/2011	12/17/2012	Yes		2.25
Koromah	THS	40%	9/28/10	$77,000	15%	5%; $495 Admin Fee	10/1/2011	7/19/2012	Yes		1.81
Marsh	SFD	35%	9/29/10	$155,000	16%	6%; $495 Admin Fee	10/1/2011	11/1/2010	Yes		0.09
McMillan/Larcheveux	SFD	60%	10/5/10	$110,000	15%	5%; $495 Admin;$450 inspection fees	11/1/2011	4/24/2013	Yes		2.55
Webster	SFD	56%	10/7/10	$101,000	15%	5%; $495 Admin;$150 Inspection Fees	10/1/2011	7/1/2011	Yes		0.73

Felton	SFD	62%	10/22/10	$125,000	15%	5%; $495 Admin Fee; $150 Inspection Fee	11/1/2011	3/5/2012	Yes		1.37
McConnell	SFD	54%	10/29/10	$112,300	13%	5%; $495 Admin; $850 Inspection fees	11/1/2011	2/17/2012	Yes		1.30
McCLoskey	WATERFRONT LOTS	56%	10/29/10	$205,000	15%	5%; $495 Admin Fee	11/1/2011	10/19/2012	No	-6,000	1.98
Linkous	SFD	50%	11/8/10	$55,000	15%	5%; $495 Inspection fees	11/1/2011	7/1/2011	Yes		0.64
Independence Properties	SFD	58%	11/8/10	$127,000	14%	5%; $950 Inspection Fees	11/1/2011	6/15/2011	Yes		0.60
Webster	SFD	49%	12/3/10	$84,000	15%	5%; $495 Admin; $300 Inspection Fees	12/1/2001	4/1/2011	Yes		0.33
Tabbs	THS	63%	12/15/10	$183,000	15%	5%; $495 Admin Fee; $600 inspection fees	1/1/2012	10/31/2013	Yes		2.88
Webster	SFD	60%	12/29/10	$77,500	15%	5.5%; $495 Admin Fee; $600 Inspection Fees	1/1/2012	5/24/2011	Yes		0.40
Webster	SFD	58%	1/4/11	$98,000	15%	5%; $495 Admin; $150 Inspection fee	1/1/2012	5/18/2011	Yes		0.37
Webster	SFD	50%	1/14/11	$88,000	15%	5%; $495 Admin; $300 Inspection Fees	2/1/2012	7/19/2011	Yes		0.51
Woodruff	SFD	65%	1/24/11	$284,000	15%	5%; $495 Admin Fee; $1300 Inspection Fees	2/1/2012	11/23/2011	Yes		0.83
Adunola	SFD	51%	2/7/11	$268,000	15%	6%; $495 Admin; $750 Inspection Fees	3/1/2012	6/9/2011	Yes		0.33
Akuffo/Sivels	THS	47%	4/4/11	$50,000	16%	6%; $495 Admin	5/1/2011	10/2/2013	No	-6,744	2.50
Tiwang	SFD	57%	4/8/11	$85,000	16%	6%; $495 Admin Fee; $950 inspection fees	4/1/2012	10/31/2011	Yes		0.56
Webster	SFD	55%	4/13/11	$88,900	15%	5%; $495 Admin; 2 Inspection Fees	5/1/2012	8/1/2011	Yes		0.30
Jovetic	THS	56%	4/18/11	$138,000	15%	6%; $495 Admin Fee; $950 inspection fees	4/1/2012	2/24/2012	Yes		0.85
Sklar	SFD	45%	4/20/11	$200,000	12%	2%; $495 Admin	4/1/2012	3/12/2012	yes		0.90
Omopariola	SFD	57%	4/22/11	$68,000	16%	6%; $495 Admin; $600 Inspection Fees	5/1/2012	8/29/2011	Yes		0.35
Adunola	THS	57%	4/26/11	$238,000	15%	5%; $595 Admin Fee	5/1/2012	5/7/2013	Yes		2.03
Manning/Mitchell	SFD	65%	4/28/11	$139,000	15%	5%; $495 Admin Fee; $600 Inspection Fees	5/1/2012	11/9/2011	Yes		0.53

Reece	SFD	60%	5/5/11	$120,000	16%	6%; $495 Admin; $450 Inspection Fees	6/1/2012	12/1/2012	No	0	1.58
Webster	SFD	64%	5/13/11	$105,000	15%	5%; $300 inspection fees	5/1/2012	12/6/2011	Yes		0.57
Webster	SFD	63%	6/2/11	$190,200	15%	5%; $300 inspection fees	6/1/2012	7/22/2011	Yes		0.14
Linkous	SFD	54%	6/21/11	$112,000	16.00%	6%; $495 Admin Fee; $600 Inspection Fee	7/1/2012	$41,748	Yes		2.83
Kennard	SFD	58%	7/22/11	$87,000	16%	6%; $495 Admin Fee; $950 inspection fees	8/1/2012	2/13/2012	Yes		0.56
Webster	SFD	52%	7/22/11	$88,000	15%	5%; $495 Admin Fee; $300 Inspection Fees	8/1/2012	3/16/2012	Yes		0.65
Webster	SFD	44%	8/1/11	$67,500	15%	5%; $495 Admin Fee; $600 Inspection Fees	8/1/2012	9/2/2011	Yes		0.09
Omopariola	SFD	57%	8/11/11	$75,000	16%	6%; $495 Admin Fee; $950 inspection fees	9/1/2012	2/21/2012	Yes		0.53
Total		54.17%		$9,552,050	14.90%					($43,696)	1.25

* fees to manager not investor; used to cover costs for the most part.

Loan pool summary:

- Total money advanced: $9,552,050
- Total number of loans: 62
- Average loan term: 1.25 years
- Total number of defaulted loans: 7 (one borrower defaulted on 3 loans)
- Total up-front fees paid: $286,561 (estimate of 3% that went to me as lender)
- Total interest collected: $1,660,464 (estimated at 14 months on average rate of 14.9%)
- Total losses on the defaulted loans: $43,096 (most of it from 1 loan)
- Gross profit on loan pool: $1,903,929 or 19.9% return unleveraged

By now, I am guessing many of you are saying to yourself "Baloney" or possibly other four letter words that suggest the above list can't be accurate. How could 62 borrowers pay an average of 14.9% interest, an average of 3% in fees per loan to the lender and do all of this at an average loan to value of 54%. Many of you might be saying: "What type of borrowers are these?" and "Why normal people would pay these very high interest rates and fees?" If we interview these borrowers, some of them who have in fact contributed to this book, you will hear the same answer. The banking system and "standard" borrowing solutions were not readily available to them and they were desiring to purchase foreclosed homes and resell them for a profit. Private lenders were the only and last option if these real estate investors wanted to attempt to buy, fix up, and re-sell the real estate for the desired profits.

Perhaps the reader believes that all these people were "deadbeats" or never paid their bills on time. While some in the list of borrowers have credit issues, none of these borrowers were in default on their mortgage at the time they borrowed money from me. It was their desire to make money using my money AND their inability to borrower from banks and financial institutions that drove them to borrower from me at these very high costs.

The great part about the above list is this…. Almost every one of these borrowers thanked me when I lent them the money and when they paid me off. In fact, many of these borrowers borrowed again on future transactions. The reality is that I allowed them to be the entrepreneur they wanted to be and leverage their capital with mine to make more capital.

Why would these borrowers not go to a bank?

There are over 13,000 banks and credit unions in this county. The question is how many of them will lend to the borrowers on the case studies in this chapter? Early in my career, in the 1980's and 1990's, my answer would have been that many community banks would have provided to at least 50% of these borrowers the loans requested, provided the property and borrower lived in their community and was a client of the bank lending the money. Today, I strongly believe that the community bank that provides the loan to a "B" grade transaction is not there to serve their community anymore. The big banks have taken over and these anti-community banks have what I call *"centralized, standardized, and de-sensitized real estate lending."* The true community bank of old does not exist. Certainly there is good argument to say that some banks provided loans to some of the wrong borrowers in the past, but I would argue that our banks today have been forced by the bank structure itself and the regulators who have to prevent bad lending, to only serve the top 40% of our borrowers. Why 40%, nothing factual, purely anecdotal on my part but the community bank can no longer take any risk. In the next chapter, I explain my position on the reason for this and it likely will create a good debate.

Then there is the other half of the borrowers who are too risky for a bank to lend. Most of these people pay their bills as agreed and have sufficient documented income to satisfy the bank's scrutiny when borrowing money. However, for many people, something in their credit or income profiles limits them from being able to borrow. When I am traveling around the United States raising money for my mortgage fund I get asked the same question: "Why would these people pay such high rates and fees?"

To summarize the above two paragraphs and explain, I will sum up the answer as such: "Half of the borrowers could get financed by a bank, but do not have the patience to find the bank and get frustrated at the timeline to borrower and the other half cannot qualify for income or credit reasons."

Our deeper dig into the case studies

Throughout this book, I repeat myself in an effort to illustrate to the reader the dynamics of our current lending and borrowing situation in the United States for a segment of our population. I have illustrated just a handful of examples out of thousands, where private lending provides a great benefit to borrowers as well as others who might indirectly benefit. OK, so let's dig just a little deeper into the examples and uncover why these people borrowed private funds, why the banks would not likely lend to these folks, and the patterns that existed within these examples.

In the previous chapters we discussed a few "key lending requirements" or guidelines that were suggested as a private lender. The perspective from the part of the borrower, lender, and perhaps a third party might conclude the list below.

From the borrower's perspective, the answer would be:

- *I could not get money from financial institutions for various reasons of credit, income, or loan types.*
- *My expected net profit, after the transactions were completed, averaged 12% of the asset, or approximately $20,000 - $25,000 on the single houses and $300,000 to $1,000,000 on multifamily deals so I could justify borrowing at the high rate and fees.*
- *My average timeline to make this profit was less than 1 year so interest rate is not important.*

- *In most of the transaction, buying and selling houses was my part time income.*
- *I was motivated to establish credit with a private lending source so I could do more transactions.*
- *I need to perform on the transaction because I had something to gain and something to lose in each deal.*

From the lender's perspective:

- *I provided a service to the borrowers/investors which borrowed money because they had a difficult time getting it from other lending institutions*
- *I earned an average of 12-14% annually in interest income*
- *My average loan to value was around 53%, whereby the capital invested was materially protected by the real estate and security instrument against the real estate.*
- *The borrowers ALL used some of their own money in the transactions putting them at risk of loss and not just the lender.*
- *The borrowers all signed a personal guarantee to repay the loan to me as private lender.*
- *I knew that the borrower wanted to complete the rehab of the homes so that the borrowers could sell them for profits and also recoup their initial investment.*

From another perspective:

- *The loan helped the buyer acquire the property, and then renovated and resold it. This improves the neighborhood we live in.*
- *The loan allowed a contractor to be working and earn money from the rehab.*
- *The loan allowed real estate and title people to earn commissions from the transaction.*
- *The loan allowed the selling bank that likely had it on its books to get the property off its books and repaid.*
- *At the end of the day, there are countless benefits from private lenders in our marketplace.*

In other words

- ❖ Borrowers benefit greatly from private lenders as illustrated in the case studies.
- ❖ The case studies suggest there is a market for the private lending sector.
- ❖ The main reasons borrowers pay high rates and fees is because they are utilizing these funds to make money.
- ❖ Most of the loans that I originated were short term renovation loans.
- ❖ The community banks previously provided funding to these types of borrowers.
- ❖ Everyone benefits from the shared capital in a successful real estate transaction.

BE THE BANK:

Chapter 6:
Basics of Underwriting Mortgage Loans

HERE'S WHAT WE COVER IN THIS CHAPTER

- **Underwriting overview – My way of thinking**
- **Underwriting the borrower**
- **Underwriting the property**
- **Chapter Summary**

UNDERWRITING OVERVIEW - MY WAY OF THINKING

What is underwriting and why is this chapter important to private mortgage lending? My answer sounds something like this:

*"Underwriting can be described as following a set of guidelines designed to **predict or eliminate** the likely default on the loan by the borrower and the risk of capital loss in the event of foreclosure."*

Certainly banks and all financial institutions want to defend against loan defaults and definitely against loss of capital. I would argue, that a private lender should defend more from loss of capital then borrower loan default. Now I know what you are thinking, you think I am saying to ignore the prediction of a loan payment default. That is not what I am saying but what I am saying is that priority number 1 should be against capital loss and priority number 2 should be against loan payment default. In the previous chapter we examined a pool of high interest rate loans and no doubt you might have had to pause and think to yourself about loan payment defaults in relation to the interest rates but in all cases when I underwrote those loans I tried to **"predict"** loan payment performance versus **"preventing"** loan payment defaults.

When I am teaching others about underwriting, I explain that underwriting is broken down into two main sections: underwriting *the borrower* and underwriting *the collateral*. Let's examine why I like to do this. Consider the variables in this table:

Mortgage loan analysis from an underwriting point of view	Likely loan performance & probability of loss
Good borrower & poor property (collateral)	Good performance & higher risk of loss if default
Poor borrower & good property (collateral)	Bad performance & lower risk of loss if default
Good borrower & good property (collateral)	Good performance & lower risk of loss if default
Poor borrower & poor property (collateral)	Bad performance & higher risk of loss if default

Let's reflect on the philosophy as private lender and then expand with the possible solutions for borrower in table below. Basically, it could be tough in 3 out of 4 scenarios for a bank to provide financing.

Underwriting description	Bank approvable?	Solution
Good borrower & poor property (collateral)	No, depends on property situation	Bank likely will not lend due to collateral but will conduct a proper evaluation of property to determine if it is marketable and sufficient to protect capital. LTV needs to be very low.
Poor borrower & good property (collateral)	No	This is a typical borrower who looks to private lenders for loans. If the probability of borrower default is high, keep LTV very low.
Good borrower & good property (collateral)	Yes	Borrower should be able to borrow at best terms from banks and will not typically need a private lender.
Poor borrower & poor property (collateral)	No	This borrower probably cannot borrow money at all, because he is likely going to default and collateral is not sufficient to support a loan from a private lender.

The point I am making here is that to be a good private lender or investor is to understand the difference between the default by a borrower and loss of capital as it relates to the underwriting of both borrower and collateral. The most profound statement I could make is that loans default because a borrower stopped making the loan payments. Yep, I told you it was profound. I am a genius I know for figuring this one out...OK, enough kidding, so let's examine why the person did default. The reasons are in the next table:

MANAGING PAYMENT
DEFAULT REASONS AND ASSOCIATED RISK

Default reason	Typical underwriting rule	Risk mitigation
Borrower does not have the income to make the payments.	Evaluate borrower's sources and the amount of income should be more than twice borrower's expenses.	Proper documentation of borrower's historical cash flow, reserves for payments during term of loan can sometimes offset cash flow.
Borrower made the decision to not pay based on priority of obligations.	Pull credit history to determine historical pattern of paying obligations and which obligations were fulfilled.	Credit scoring models have figured this one out for the most part. Historical credit patterns typically determine future pay patterns.
Borrower has a physical or psychological life event that determines the borrower to not remember or just to not pay.	Tough to underwrite to this life event.	Loan default mitigation on this one is almost impossible, with the exception of collecting of payments in reserves and having multiple people on the hook
Borrower becomes deceased.	Tough to underwrite to this event.	Unless you can predict death or know health of borrower at time of loan closing, it could be tough to mitigate.
Borrower NO longer has a benefit to keep the asset.	Always insure that borrower has financial gain and/or loss should he or she default or lose property.	Cash from borrower invested in transaction and a substantial amount of equity upon sale typically presents this default reason.

UNDERWRITING FOCUS AREA # 1:
UNDERWRITING THE BORROWER

In previous chapters we discussed that we need to look at the borrower's "profile" to determine payment default risk. What I mean by "profile" is the borrower's ***ability and willingness*** to repay the loan. Underwriting the borrower's focus in on the loan payment default risk allows the lender to conclude if the borrower has the documented income to afford the new loan and all the existing payment obligations and also has the credit history and credit use patterns to want to make the payments. "Ability" & "Desire" to pay the loan back is what we are looking for here.

Does the borrower have the ability to repay me?

As a private lender, you want to review the "ability to repay" documentation in a very similar way to banks and other financial institutions. The typical bank and non-bank income & asset documentation requirements are listed below:

- Tax returns for the previous 2 years (personal & business)
- W2s for the previous 2 years (if applicable)
- Pay stubs for the last 30 days
- Bank statements for the last 12 months (non-traditional argument)
- Personal financial statements (list of assets and liabilities)
- Most recent reports on all liquid assets from PFS

Traditional underwriting for most loan applications consists in reviewing the gross incomes for the past 2 years and determining the borrower's affordability, based on the average income amount and the length of time on the job and determines if the borrower can afford the payment. I personally prefer to look at bank statements to see the average deposits and average expenses each month and compare them with tax returns. Often the applications do not catch the patterns of income or expenses like bank statements do. As a private lender I like to average the deposits in bank statements for self-employed borrowers as I have found this to be a better indicator of gross income averages and expense averages. I also like to look at the borrower's reserves or liquid assets when assessing the loan. If I think a borrower might not be able to afford a payment, the amount of liquid assets can help support the decision when trying to predict the ability to repay and the default risk. A good underwriter will review the patterns of income generated, patterns of expenses, patterns of savings, and historical ability to earn income.

Questions I like to ask regarding income and assets are:

o   Has the borrower filed their tax returns for the past 3 years?

o   Has the borrower jumped around from job to job?

o   Is the borrower in a stable profession?

o   Has the borrower's income been consistent for the past 3 years?

o   Is the borrower's income increasing or decreasing?

o   Does the borrower only have one source of income or multiple sources?

o   Do the borrowers have at least 12 months of payment reserves?

o   Do the borrowers show a pattern of reserves?

o   Do the bank statements support the income stated?

o   Do the bank statements reflect a pattern of over spending?

o   Can my borrower afford the payment even if they need to utilize reserves to make the payment?

o   Since the applications typically do not cover items such as school tuitions & day to day living expenses, do the bank statements reflect a borrower robbing Peter to pay Paul?

Does the borrower have the willingness & character to repay me?

Now this section is on credit or what I like to describe is the borrower's *character* to repay the debt. In my opinion, life events happen each day that can cause a possible interruption of income, fluctuation of income, or ability to repay. All of us, as lenders, do our best to predict if the borrower has the character to not default on the loan they just borrowed from our company. The credit profile usually tells a story, especially if it is a long profile or credit report. In this section I am sure I can get pretty strange when speaking about credit reports or credit scores in the same discussion as someone's "character" or "personal integrity", but the reality is that most of us have faced bad times in our life, either financially or physically or even psychologically, but we chose to pay our bills or obligations on time regardless of the circumstance. "Now wait a minute Ben." I hear you saying. "That is bull crap. I lost my job and I did not have the income to pay my bills as agreed." Perhaps a job was lost and the credit suffered but what we would see in the borrower's profile is a good pattern until the job was lost and then a pattern of recovery after. The reality is when I underwrite credit properly I can see a list of patterns that will likely predict the future payment patterns. Credit scoring has replaced the old school need to predict this, however, as an old school underwriter I wanted to teach the private lender how to additionally look at the patterns and supplement the credit score reviews as another determination of willingness to pay. Let's break down the credit review into two parts: **expense patterns and repayment patterns.**

The typical credit and expense documentation

- Single bureau or tri merged credit report for all borrowers
- Copies of cancelled checks for housing and other payments
- Criminal background report on borrowers
- Judgement report on borrowers
- Bank statements for the lase 12 months to show expenses & patterns

I find credit review to be an interesting topic. The reason is that information on a credit report can be aged, recent or not exist, so judging the patterns of credit can often be challenging. As a private lender I look for historical credit patterns and recent trends that could give me a lot of trouble after closing. I realize credit scores exist today and these scores are designed to predict default, but let's consider the "old school" approach of asking some questions listed below.

Questions I ask regarding credit profile are:

o   Does the borrower have a pattern of not paying as agreed?
o   Do the delinquencies reflect a slow payer or severe delinquency?
o   If yes to question 1, how delinquent is the pattern of delinquency? Meaning does the borrower have only slow pays of 60 day or less or has the borrower allowed accounts to go to judgment?
o   Has the borrower ever defaulted on a mortgage?
o   Are the defaults for a specific time period?
o   Were the credit issues caused by a "recurring or non-recurring life event?" Was the life event that caused the credit issue documented?

o   Is the borrower's high credit consistent with their loan request? In other words, if you are considering lending them 1 million and they have never borrowed more than 100k that is an issue because they have not demonstrated their ability to handle that high amount.

o   Has the borrower consistently utilized close to 100% of the available credit?

o   Does the borrower have available credit to draw from after closing in case of emergency? If yes, how much is available?

Some key indicators of character review from a credit profile are:

• A credit profile of the past usually reflects the future so a borrower with a past credit problem typically means they are likely to have future credit problems.

• A credit profile that shows no pattern of poor credit, just a "period" of poor credit, should be documented to find evidence if there is a life event issue. This is typically a good borrower who experienced a bad period of time. As a private lender, this borrower could have been turned down by a bank that cannot look past the life event. I love this type of borrower, because the borrower will likely perform on the loan provided the life event does not reoccur.

• A borrower who is willing to allow multiple accounts to go all the way to collection & judgement is NOT the same as a borrower who has 30 and 60 days late payments regardless of the number of late payments. Without getting off track here, sub-prime lending is and was a very good business and idea, provided the lender sticks to the "slow payers" versus what I call the "defaulters".

• I often teach about the credit curve or credit report curve meaning that if a borrower has recently utilized all his or her credit, they look great in the profile, but the credit history was not very long and they might have utilized the credit to the max and are now about to default. This is how some of the lenders can get misguided by good credit because the history is good and the profile is good but the credit has been used up and the borrower is at the point of default.

Very difficult to defend against even though credit scores consider available credit.

Credit scores in the US as published by FICO in the table below suggest that 1/3 of the population has less than good credit as indicated in red. If most banks are only lending to borrowers with credit scores above 650, then consider that 34% or 1/3 of all borrowers might have to use a non-bank for financing.

FICO Score Distribution by Percentage of Population

FICO Score	2005	2006	2007	2008	2009	2010	2011	2012	2013
300-499	6.6%	6.5%	7.1%	7.2%	7.4%	6.9%	6.2%	6.0%	5.8%
500-549	8.0%	8.0%	8.0%	8.2%	8.7%	9.0%	8.7%	8.5%	8.4%
550-599	9.0%	8.8%	8.7%	8.7%	9.1%	9.6%	9.8%	9.9%	9.8%
600-649	10.2%	10.2%	9.7%	9.6%	9.5%	9.5%	10.0%	10.1%	10.2%
650-699	12.8%	12.5%	12.1%	12%	11.9%	11.9%	12.1%	12.2%	12.7%
700-749	16.4%	16.3%	16.2%	16%	15.9%	15.7%	15.5%	16.2%	16.3%
750-799	20.1%	19.8%	19.8%	19.6%	19.4%	19.5%	19.4%	18.8%	18.4%
800-850	16.9%	17.9%	18.4%	18.7%	18.2%	17.9%	18.3%	18.4%	18.6%
Total	100%	100%	100%	100%	100%	100%	100%	100%	100%

Underwriting the borrower conclusion

As a private lender, we want to do our best to determine if we believe the borrower will default based on documented and argued ability to afford the payments and if the borrower has demonstrated the historical willingness for making the payments to creditors. Most private lenders receive business because the borrowers were turned down by their banks due to issues with affordability or credit documentation or past loan performance. As we mentioned in previous chapters, banks cannot take any payment default risks and therefore many opportunities exist for the private lender. "Hard money" lenders do not typically care about affordability or credit profile because at the end of the day the collateral will protect the capital. What I like to teach is that regardless of the property protecting the capital, every private lender should understand the borrower's profile so that loan structure, rate of return, default and collection projections are managed. I have often said in credit committee meetings to my underwriters or bankers: *"What is the likely chance this borrower defaults and why?"* I sometimes use a default scale of 1-10 or use percentages of default on chances of default so that I can price and structure the loan accordingly. At the end of this chapter we will summarize the relationship of the loan default scale to the pricing and loan to value.

UNDERWRITING FOCUS AREA # 2: UNDERWRITING THE PROPERTY

Does the collateral properly protect my capital advanced to borrower?

Previously in this chapter we explained that underwriting was broken up into 2 parts: underwriting the borrower and underwriting the collateral or property. Throughout this chapter we use the word "property" and "collateral" interchangeably so when we say one, we are also saying the other in the same context. In chapter 4 we covered property types and key questions that should be asked and answered about making mortgage loans and what a private lender should ask before lending the money. What we want to do in this section of the chapter is to dig deeper into decision-making or underwriting of the collateral securing the loan. I realize that throughout this book I repeat myself but it in an effort to reinforce the belief system and success formula that I have mastered as a private lender. My objective as chief credit officer for the Fund I manage is to first make sure that regardless of all else, the collateral or property that the loan is securing will protect the capital advanced on the loan. So as Will Rogers said so well: "The return of the money is more important than the return on the money." I could not agree more with this statement and it holds true to how a private lender should think when making loan decisions. Banks underwrite to insure there are NO borrower defaults and I underwrite to ensure there is no capital loss therefore underwriting the collateral is actually more important to me than underwriting the borrower. Don't get me wrong, underwriting both the borrower and property are important, but what happens in the off chance the borrower defaults? I need to know that my capital investment is covered. OK, so what do we do to insure we have underwritten the property?

To determine if the capital is in fact protected, several factors need to be considered: Consider the following:

1. Loan-to-value – What should the maximum be to protect capital?
2. Property type – Given the type of property, who will purchase the property if I foreclose?
3. Property condition – What will I need to fix or renovate to sell it if I foreclose?
4. Property location – Is the property in an urban or rural location or a location that would have an effect on the sale and marketability if I foreclose?
5. Marketing time – Based on questions # 1-4 above how long will it take for me to recover my capital if I foreclose?
6. Capital amount advanced – At the end of the review what is the safe amount I should advance to protect my capital? A 2 million loan might be harder to collect on then a $200,000 loan.

Most lenders require a standard list when it comes to the review of the collateral. The variations of the documentation has to do with what type of property is being secured, the size of the loan, and the requirements by each lender.

The typical collateral documentation:

- Recent appraisal by an experienced licensed appraiser
- On-line comps from Zillow, Trulia, Realtor.com, etc.
- Opinion by local real estate agent
- On-site property inspection by company personnel
- On a purchase copy of the purchase contract
- Property ownership history
- Feasibility study (specific to certain properties)
- Environmental study (specific to certain properties)

Every bank I know requires an appraisal before making a loan decision. The appraisal represents an opinion of value that is supported by the data in the appraisal. You might say it is an "argument of value." I often ask my staff how good is the argument of value. In previous chapters we discussed "*value range*" vs "*a value*" because in most cases the various comparable sales used by the appraiser represent different sale prices or arguments of value that are compared so to me a range of value is more appropriate. In addition to an appraisal, there are other third party reports or information that can be obtained to conclude the value range and marketability of the subject property.

Since this book is focused on the readers learning how to invest in mortgages, mortgage pools, a mortgage fund, or just become his or her own private lender, I should just focus on the key areas to manage when it comes to values or value ranges. These key areas that all private lenders should focus on include:

o How many homes are considered in the immediate marketplace? Urban areas should have a ton; suburban should be within 3 miles and preferably 1 mile and rural areas should be within 5 miles, preferably 3 miles or less.

o How many homes are for sale in the immediate marketplace that are similar to our subject?

o Is the housing inventory over 6 months? 9 months? 12 months or longer?

o How many homes have sold in the past 6 months in the immediate marketplace?

o What was the average marketing time for comps in appraisal and other data reviewed? Was it over 90 days? 180 days is considered a potential problem?

o What is the value range of the houses that are similar that are sold and listed within the immediate marketplace?

o Did the appraiser only use the "best" argument of these sales or the "entire or bracketed" argument? New appraisal rules now require the appraiser to provide all the data.

o Can you still get 100% of your capital back, including foreclosure expenses utilizing the low end of value range of collateral?

o Are proper adjustments made for condition and location of the collateral?

o Did you perform a site inspection of collateral personally to confirm the value range makes sense to you?

o When sitting at the road staring at the property, did you feel comfortable with the neighborhood and believe that a homeowner would want to purchase the home?

o Did you see any boarded up homes on the block or in the immediate neighborhood?

o Did you see an external or internal obsolescence to the collateral, such as a house sitting right next to the railroad tracks or airport, or the layout of the home was dysfunctional and not conducive for a family to use properly?

o   Did you speak with an experienced real estate broker that sells homes in the immediate neighborhood?

o   Does the appraiser for the subject property live and work in the same area as the property that was appraised? My fund requires the appraiser to live within 30 miles of the subject.

o   If I wanted to sell the home within 60 days, what would the likely sale price need to be and what amount of money would I need to spend to get the home in the condition to sell?

o   One of the questions I used to ask is what is the predicted real estate market appreciation over the next 12-24-36 months? For obvious reasons I do not ask this question anymore instead I ask what the market increase is or decrease over the next 12-24 months is expected to be?

Purchase money loans

We discussed underwriting the borrower and also underwriting the collateral as the main focus. On purchase transactions you will want to also underwrite the purchase. When a borrower is purchasing a property there are a few very specific questions that a private lender should ask:

o   Is there a related party between buyer and seller?

o   Is the seller holding a 2nd mortgage?

o   Did the seller take the title within the past 6 months?

o   Is the seller actually on title?

o   Is there a documented deposit with the contract?

o   Is the seller a private party or a company?

o   Is the contract buyer an assignee or was the contract signed?

o   Do I have a copy of the ownership history for the past 2 years?

It would likely take a complete chapter to cover the details surrounding the above list, so the reader should just be aware of these questions and make sure the answers are known and that common sense should apply. What you as the lender are worried about is fraud between the buyer and seller or between the buyer and an appraiser. Often, a lender assumes that the contract price is properly argued and documented because a buyer has agreed to pay that price, however until that contract and price is properly vetted it could be materially off. I have many examples in my career where the buyer and the seller got together to create an inflated price so the lender would lend off that inflated contract price only to learn that the contract price was make believe and materially higher than on the market.

Underwriting the collateral conclusion

As I have stated over and over again, the key to not losing money as a private lender is to know your collateral. For this reason, private lenders should lend in markets they are familiar with, property types they understand, and have a first-hand knowledge of the subject collateral in case of a default. Obtaining third party reports, performing a personal site visit, speaking with the local real estate broker, and concluding a value range is the key to underwriting the collateral. Property condition and external factors should play a role in adjusting downward or upward the value range on each deal. Do not rely on the top value range only as markets shift.

Consider the chart below from Robert Shiller's book as published also in the NY times on home values from 1890. **Counting** on real estate adjusted for inflation to increase in value is not a smart move by any lender and in fact, many lenders now should consider a decline in value and make decisions based on that possibility.

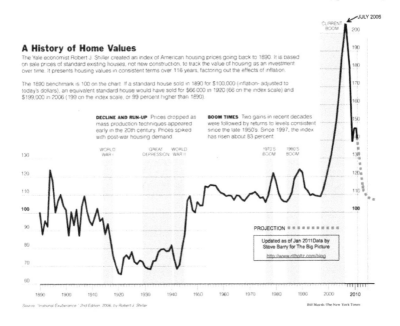

In other words

- ❖ Most banks and lenders view underwriting as decision making in support of a no-default borrower.
- ❖ My definition of underwriting is more of the prediction of a likely default.
- ❖ Underwriting the borrower focuses on ability and willingness to pay.
- ❖ Ability to repay is determined by the borrower's affordability of **all** payments.
- ❖ Willingness to repay demonstrates the borrower's character.
- ❖ Underwriting the collateral focuses on protecting the capital advanced.
- ❖ Borrowers can be slow pays but good risk to lend.
- ❖ There are variations of good vs. bad borrowers and collateral which have a role in the decision process.
- ❖ Perform your own review of collateral as a private lender.
- ❖ Do not expect real estate values to increase.

BE THE BANK:

Chapter 7:
Comparing Banks vs. Private Lenders

HERE'S WHAT WE COVER IN THIS CHAPTER

- **The role of a private lender**
- **Reviewing the bank's restrictions today in mortgage lending**
- **The "Risk Classes" of lending**
- **Chapter Summary**

LET'S TALK ABOUT PRIVATE
MORTGAGE LENDING AND RELATE IT TO OUR BANKS

The book is called **"Be the Bank"** for a reason. Historically and today, the banks or mortgage bankers in the United States represent the majority of all lenders providing mortgage loans.

In this chapter I want to explain the role of a private lender in our country, but in order to do this I wanted to compare what a private mortgage lender does versus what a bank does and wanted to explain that when most people look to borrow money secured by an investment property, they turn to their local, regional, or national bank. Since my career began, I have watched the community banks either fail or be gobbled up by larger banks. I have either been working *with*, working *for* or been a *shareholder* in many banks in my career and I am saddened by the historical events such as the savings and loan crisis of the mid 1980's and the financial collapse of 2007-2009. 30 years ago there were approximately 15,000 banks and today there are less than 7500, or half the number. Perhaps this is a good thing or perhaps it's not, but one thing

I know is that for various reasons banks cannot survive any type of negative market shift or take on any type of risk to their balance sheet given the current financial structure of most of our banks.

My opinion is the sub-prime lending, the no-income documented loan, the 100% loan-to-value loan, all created the financial collapse, as these wrong lending guidelines contributed to the wrong borrowers having access to mortgage capital. This access to the capital artificially drove up home prices for a period of time until the loan performance of these borrowers started to show that they could not make the payments and then the entire "house of cards" came down. My opinion is that from 2003-2007 this house of cards was created by providing the wrong borrowers with loans and the increase in home prices masked the risk until enough of the loans defaulted in 2006 & 2007. So what is different about being a private lender vs. what happened in 2003-2007? What is the relationship between what happened in sub-prime, what banks provide as mortgage loans, and what a private lender does?

Lender	Lending philosophy	Capital risk if default
Banks today	Only lend to high credit score, and full income, low loan to value	Lower risk of default but likely lose 20% of capital on defaulted loan.
Sub-prime lender 2003-2007	Allowed credit scores down to 580, allowed no-income to be documented, loaned 100% of the value of property	High risk of default and likely lose 30-50% of capital if default
Private Lender	All credit scores considered, should show ability to repay loan, only lends at low loan-to-values	Depending on borrower profile moderate risk of default and likely 5-20% risk to capital depending on loan-to-values

I have, throughout this book, commented on the banking system in this country and often I like to pontificate on the subject and I become unpopular especially with many bankers and perhaps regulators who prefer to take an opposing position. The bankers take the position because they are in an industry that says risk of default cannot be tolerated so therefore a "no risk" approach is made. I completely agree that this is the right approach given our banking capital structure today, but there is a contradiction going on with the regulations. The regulators require a bank to comply with the community reinvestment act and other lending goals of allowing small business to borrow money, but then the bank gets criticized for making a loan where someone defaults. It is a balancing act that requires walking the exact line between lending enough money and not making a mistake to the wrong borrower. Keep in mind that when I speak about banking I am referring to the concept that most small banks generate the majority of their income from making loans. Let me explain how a typical community bank balance sheet is structured. Please note that I am simplifying this example.

Balance Sheet (Dollars in Millions)	Current Period	Prior Period
Assets		
Federal Funds sold and securities purchased under agreements to resell	$176,922	$157,274
Residential mortgage	$178,359	$188,846
Credit card	$98,022	$92,207
Direct/Indirect consumer	$119,920	$105,048
Commercial	$110,163	$101,097
Total loans and leases	$683,386	$644,472
Other earning assets	$39,112	$37,924
Total earning assets	$722,498	$682,396
Cash and cash equivalents	$32,575	$30,558
Allowance for loan and lease losses	$79,854	$80,837
Total assets	**$834,927**	**$793,791**
Liabilities		
Domestic interest-bearing deposits		
Savings	$39,056	$37,275
Now and money market deposit accounts	$236,564	$223,376
CDs and time deposits	$134,799	$121,456
Total interest-bearing deposits	$410,420	$382,107
Federal funds purchased, securities sold under agreements to repurchase and other short-term borrowings	$128,171	$116,002
Long-term debt	$76,037	$76,934
Total interest-bearing liabilities	$614,628	$575,043
Non-interest-bearing liabilities	$148,101	$144,901
Shareholder's equity	$72,198	$73,847
Total liabilities and shareholders equity	**$834,927**	**$793,791**

Not to digress too much but banks are considered "well capitalized" if they have 8%-10% Tier 1 capital. This means in a nutshell that if a bank has 90% debt (either from depositors or borrowed funds), that they only need 10% equity to be considered a well-capitalized bank. I am sure those bankers that are reading this are saying this is not the exact formula for the capital calculation and I do agree that this is not exact. Banks do a risk weight on certain assets and this changes the exact formula and calculation of capital as percentage for leverage purposes and leverage calculations, but I am using an approximate example to illustrate my point.

Often, the majority of a community bank's assets are invested in loans so the bank inherently cannot take *ANY* risks on *ANY* level because they do not have enough equity capital should the borrowers default.

So what am I proposing here?

The private lender exists because certain borrowers cannot gain access to the low cost of bank loans. Are these the borrowers that should not be loaned money to? My entire thesis is centered on a different view of how lenders and borrowers can benefit and that banks will only serve a certain segment of borrower as a result of the risk that a bank can take. Perhaps certain community banks could have a different business model where they have much more capital and expand their lending reach to many more borrowers looking for loans. I understand that the FDIC is insuring the depositors against loss should the bank go under but a balance between more capital and insurance would likely expand what I call the **"No risk"** policy to **"A variation risk"** policy. I also realize that the regulators have a "risk weighting" based on asset class, however if we are focusing on real estate secured loans that are held for investment than the formula could possibly work. See the balance sheets below as my example of what I am suggesting.

No-risk bank

Assets	Liabilities
Loan assets totaling 70-80% of assets. LTV are high and credit requirements narrow.	Total bank debts are 80-90%, mostly from depositors.
	Total capital by bank is 10-20%

Variation risk bank (lender)

Assets	Liabilities
Loan assets totaling 70-80% of assets. Credit standards are wider. There are more clients with lower LTV.	Total bank debts are 80-90% mostly from depositors.
	Total capital by bank is 25-33%

The tables suggest that by adjusting the amount of capital or equity and lowering the capital exposure to a segment of borrowers (as in lower loan-to-values) it would be possible to take on additional loan risk without risking additional capital.

This book is mainly about bringing the average investor into private lending as a mainstream investment vs. something that only our banks consider. It is my hope that through this argument of "variation risk" underwriting we open up mortgage lending from banks and non-banks in a different way just like what was intended with sub-prime except that what happened with sub-prime was that the "geniuses" missed several key elements of underwriting in their models. If the credit and affordability levels are low then it should be a corresponding adjustment of lower loan-to-values and higher borrower equity exposures. I can hear you now saying: "Here he goes again talking about underwriting one minute then jumps into variation risk and sub-prime, and now he talks about banks." Let me try to pull these thoughts together.

All lending companies, whether regulated or non-regulated, will originate the loans according to a set of guidelines that support their lending goals. As we mentioned in previous chapters, companies differ on their underwriting guidelines, however they are all the same in that the underwriting guidelines are designed to support and defend against default risk. Banks for example, have NO tolerance for default risks and at the other end of the lending spectrum might be "hard money" lenders that actually expect defaults but can rely solely on the collateral to prevent capital losses. Why would or could these hard money lenders still provide capital to high default risk borrowers and feel they are making a good business decision? If a high risk borrower can borrow money for a worthwhile purpose and benefit from the use of the money, it makes sense for both lender and borrower to conduct business. We are NOT speaking about lending to owner occupied borrowers or borrowers for **consumer loans**. We are strictly speaking about **business or commercial loans**. There is a place for consumer lending that is more risky but we can talk about that another time.

I often speak about this topic in regards of underwriting and drone on about risk and risk-adjusted decisions. For example, let's relate the underwriting of mortgage loans to the grading of bonds. The theories are that an AAA rated bond will have substantially less risk of default than a BB rated bond. The reasons are attributed to the characteristics that make up the underlying collateral and risk of loss to the bond investor. The FDIC, Federal Reserve, and the OCC want a bank to manage against a no default policy and the underwriting, guidelines, policies and procedures must be very effective in managing this no loan default risk. Regulated financial institutions policies and guidelines can only support low risk tolerance or let's say AAA bond scenario so that begs the question about loans that fall outside these guidelines.

I know that I am describing the exact reason an individual is not their own bank. Will individuals have the background and lending experience to know the difference? As I go back and digest the questions asked throughout my travels on raising money, such as: "Why are individuals not the bank to borrowers?" or "Why are there not many private lenders?" it often comes down to the perception and likely reality that there are many risks that have to be managed in private lending. Even successful bankers and investors do not have the background and experience to provide mortgage loans as a private lender as it would require you, the lender, to feel comfortable that you understand all the areas where something could go wrong and cost you the loss of capital.

To conclude why banks should not take risks and why or how private lenders can lend based on a variation risk model, the table below outlines the variations or variables that can allow a private lender to make the loan and still provide a value to the borrower and protect the capital. By the way, this concept has been around for many years however my opinion is that the Wall Street bankers who tried to act on this missed the boat because they never made mortgage loans by themselves. They purchased loans based on historical or theoretical models that were flawed. Consider what would have happened in the years leading up to 2007 if the "marginal borrowers" were only allowed to borrow up to 70% loan-to-value or if all borrowers had to show cash in every loan. The sub-prime business would have worked if the worse the "borrower profile" the lower the exposure by the lender or more equity for the borrower to lose.

Let's view the table below as "risk classes" and consider the LTV, credit profile, and affordability variations that determine what class or variation of risk exists with making the loan. Defaults and capital losses are the result of these variations, in a similar way to bonds.

Loan to Value	Credit profile	Affordability	Capital loss risk	Chance of default	Pricing of loan
90-100% of value	Excellent	Excellent	If default, loss could be high	Low	High as a result of the high LTV exposure
80-90% of value	Excellent	Excellent	If default, loss could be high	Low	If 80% pricing would be very low rising up to 90%
80% of value	Very good	Very good	If default, loss will be moderate	Somewhat low	Pricing driven by credit and affordability scale
70% of value	Good	Good	If default, loss will be minimal	Possible	Pricing driven by credit and affordability scale but likely higher
60% of value	Historically slow payer	Marginally documented	If default, loss will likely be very minimal	Possible	Likely higher than market
50% of value or lower	Poor	Cannot show ability to repay loan	If default, loss will not likely occur	Possible or highly likely	Likely much higher than market

I talked earlier in this chapter about different bond ratings or classes. Mortgage underwriting can also be grouped into classes based on the risks we chose to allow. We want to focus our attention on our *loan repayment* and *loss of capital risk only when creating these classes or risk classes*. This is why I underwrite loans to first determine the "risk of loss to capital" then to the "payment default" and that I can properly classify the loan and the corresponding interest rate or return on investment.

Bottom line is the banks focus on loan defaults first and private lenders focus on capital loss first.

In conclusion, another way for me to say it is that prior to 2007, Wall Street focused on loan performance or default modeling and pushed loan-to-values too high. The banks are focusing on making sure the borrower will not default on the loan payments by carefully reviewing the credit and affordability profiles of the borrower and ensuring the collateral protects them. Private lenders take a slightly different approach as Wall Street or banks did by asking what does the credit profile suggest about the borrower's historical pattern of default and does the borrower have the income to repay the loan. If the credit and income arguments are marginal, it is important if the collateral will protect the capital under almost every circumstance.

Banks = no default risk because Capital is highly leveraged and LTV is typically high

Private lenders = can take default risk because Capital is not highly leveraged and LTV is typically low

Chapter Summary

- ❖ The role of a private lender is to provide capital to a borrower who benefits from borrowing money, where banks may not be able or agree to lend.
- ❖ Banks are required to have a "no risk model" and cannot take on borrower loan default risk at all due to the capital leverage structure.
- ❖ The financial crisis of 2008 was caused by sub-prime lending guidelines that were severely flawed
- ❖ A Variation Risk model would allow a bank with more capital and low LTV guidelines to take on slightly higher borrower default risks thus expanding available loans to borrowers.
- ❖ A possibly higher delinquency would occur at the bank in this class of loan but the loan to values would be much lower and interest rate spreads would be higher.
- ❖ Private lenders can take on more risk of default because the LTV are normally lower than a bank and the capital percentage is higher.

BE THE BANK:

Chapter 8:
Do it on your Own or Invest in a Mortgage Fund?

HERE'S WHAT WE COVER IN THIS CHAPTER

- Should you become your own private lender?
- An organized way to be your own private lender.
- Should you invest in a mortgage pool or fund?
- How to evaluate a mortgage fund
- Chapter Summary

Should I become my own private mortgage lender or should I invest in a mortgage fund?

I like to use stories about my past investing experiences to teach others, especially if they are bad experiences. Sometimes when we make mistakes, we get all upset and it stops us from keeping our feet moving forward. As a mortgage banker and private lender, self-employed since the age of 21 years, I have made my share of bad loan decisions while operating mortgage-banking firms. If you knew how many bad decisions I have made in 31 years, you might be asking yourself how I can give advice in this book on succeeding in private mortgage lending. My answer is that I have produced, directly or indirectly, over twenty thousand mortgages and over five thousand mortgages held in portfolio to service. Historically, somewhere around 4% of the mortgages I was responsible for originating went into a payment default and about .5% went to foreclosure, so over my career, there were many loans, but as a percentage, it does not seem so bad. The reason is that it really feels bad when you have to write-off 25% of your loan balance because the collateral was not worth near what you thought it would appraise for when you went to recover capital.

Doing it on your own can be very rewarding, provided the early mistakes are kept to a minimum. Mortgage lending can be a tough business where mistakes can be costly, but the possible income and returns can far outweigh the negatives.

I have several friends who are now private lenders and I would want to say that I inspired them to leave their law profession to focus on lending money as a result of the great opportunity that exists but perhaps it had nothing to do with me. The idea of having several million dollars earning 12% plus the collection of points up front allows for a very compelling business model, regardless of doing it on your own or through a fund. Almost anyone including these two friends would say: "This is the easiest business in the world, why doesn't everybody do it?" For many, the idea of lending money and charging fees and interest seems easy and natural and to others it is very risky and scary. This book attempts to convince you that lending money is neither too hard nor too easy, but something that can be learned by everyone and the rewards can be fantastic.

So we return to the question of doing it on your own or investing in a mortgage pool or fund. My short answer is it depends on how much money you have available to invest. If it is only enough to do a handful of loans, I would invest in a pool or a fund. If you have a larger amount of say, 2-3 million dollars and you want to build and manage your own mortgage portfolio, you can learn what to do on your own or with the help of experienced individuals like me.

As we begin this chapter let me organize the question and possible answers of "do it on your own" or "invest in a fund" into a chart with my pros and cons to the question.

Pros & cons	Do it on your own as private lender	Invest in a mortgage pool or fund
Pro	If you want to be your own investment manager and manage a business of lending money this is a way to do it.	Allows an investor to invest in mortgages without having to work the business.
Pro	Allows an investor to control all loan decisions	The fund manager likely will be more experienced than you managing mortgage assets
Pro	Perhaps you do better job than the mortgage fund manager	Allows for much more diversity if the mortgage fund is invested in many more assets rather than doing it on your own.
Pro or Con	Likely will cost more than investing in mortgage fund to do it on your own	Fund investors will absorb the overall cost of the fund which could be more over time than doing it yourself
Pro & Con	Likely cannot deploy leverage to loans	Leverage could produce excellent yields or excess risk depending on market & leverage rate
Pro & Con	Could take you a long time to learn the business and you could lose investment opportunities	Could invest immediately and earn income immediately

Let's review both sides of this question of doing it on your own as a private mortgage investor or just simply giving the funds to another party to invest. If you did focus on becoming a mortgage investor on your own what resources would you need and what information should you know? I realize we have discussed many of these topics in previous chapters, but in this chapter I wanted to organize it again for you. The list below is intended to be an organized guide or list of what you can do to become a private mortgage investor.

A DEEPER DIVE INTO DOING IT ON YOUR OWN

Resources & Actions required to becoming a Private Lender

1. Create your lending guidelines to include the details I addressed in previous chapters:
   a. The mortgage types
   b. The property types
   c. The geographic locations
   d. The interest rates desired
   e. The loan duration or term
   f. The loan size minimums and maximums
   g. The borrower credit profiles
   h. The borrower income profiles
   i. The collection and default terms
   j. The loan documentation
   k. The appraisal & title insurance requirements
   l. Determine if you are going to perform a site inspection to each property
   m. If you are going to provide construction or rehab money you will need specific lending criteria and documentation
   n. Any underwriting criteria not covered above
2. Locate an attorney to perform loan closings and document preparation for you.
3. Locate the same or different attorney to provide title insurance or locate a title company.
4. Determine if the state you are lending in has licensing requirements to do the type of loans you want to originate. Many states do not require a license to originate commercial loans but most if not all of them require a license if you are providing consumer loans.
5. Setup or establish an accounting system.
6. Setup a loan servicing system if more than a few loans are managed.
7. Get your Mastermind group lined up to include:
   a. A closing and real estate attorney experienced with private lenders
   b. An insurance company lined up in case you need forced place insurance
   c. A title company lined up for a title insurance policy
   d. Several appraisers in the area you will lend

    e.   Several environmental companies in case you decide to lend on industrial or manufacturing properties

    f.   Several contractors in case you need to fix up property in event of foreclosure

    g.   A collection attorney in event you have to foreclose

8.   Determine how you will market for the loans you want

Now that you have reviewed the basic requirements, if you are to do it on your own as a private lender, perhaps some of you are rethinking this a bit. The list looks long and quite frankly it is a lot to digest and learn, but the rewards are worth it to the person that commits sufficient time to learning the business.

Why not just turn my money over to a mortgage fund manager? Well, if you are like me where you have a hard time trusting others with your hard-earned money, I can understand why an investor would want to do it on his own. One of the main reasons for an investor to "do it on his own" is if the investor is looking for an active business venture versus a passive investment. For me, banking and mortgage investing has been what I do for a living, but it also is what I do with part of my retirement and non-retirement investment funds. For the person who is looking for a part time business or just wants to manage "actively" a business then becoming a private mortgage investor makes sense.

We discussed in detail what number 1 above on the list covers in chapters 2 and 4, so I will refer you to those chapters to expand on the details and significance of the loan and property types. We should however, cover some of the list in more detail so that a better understanding of the list can be provided.

Lending guidelines & Matrix – If you are planning to become a private mortgage lender as a main business versus just a few loans every now and then I would strongly suggest writing out lending guidelines and create a matrix. This will allow you to have a roadmap to follow and should you obtain loans from mortgage or real estate brokers you can provide them information on what you lend on and how you determine what loans you want to approve.

See the table of contents for the lending guidelines of the Fund that I manage and also our loan matrix.

Bridge Loan Program
Revised: February 20, 2014

Program Overview 3
   1.01 Program Overview 3
   1.02 Approval Requirements 3
   1.03 Program Matrix 3
Collateral Requirements 4
   2.01 Eligible Properties 4
   2.02 Ineligible Properties 4
   2.03 Business Plan for Property Improvements 4
   2.04 Determination of Property Value 5
   2.05 Appraisal Requirements 6
   2.06 Appraisal Review Requirements 7
   2.07 Deferred Appraisals 7
   2.08 Site Inspection Visits 7
   2.09 Cross-Collateralization 8
   2.10 Environmental Review & Remediation 8
   2.11 Property Taxes 8
   2.12 Sale History & Purchase Contracts 9
   2.13 Zoning 9
Borrower Requirements 10
   3.01 Eligible Borrowers 10
   3.02 Borrower Legal Documentation 10
Guarantor Requirements 10
   4.01 Personal Guarantees & Recourse 10
   4.02 Guarantor Legal Documentation 10
   4.03 Guarantor Experience & Resumes 10
Credit Requirements 11
   5.01 Credit Report Requirements 11
   5.02 Mortgage Debt 11
   5.03 Lawsuits, Collections, and Judgments 11
   5.04 Bankruptcies & Foreclosures 12
Ability to Repay 13
   6.01 Ability to Repay Requirements 13
   6.02 Income Documentation Requirements 13
   6.03 Financial Statements 13

First Lien Bridge Loan Program
Updated: December 9, 2015

	Single-Unit Residential	Multi-Unit Residential	Commercial (Retail, Office, Mixed Use)
Existing Construction (Renovation or Rehabilitation)			
Maximum LTV (based on "as completed" value)	70%	70%	65%
Maximum Initial Advance (for construction loans)	**Bank REO or Distressed Sale** Limited to the lesser of: · 90% of the purchase price (if a purchase) · 90% of the "as is" appraised value · Maximum loan amount minus cost to complete **Non-Distressed Sale or Refinance** Limited to the lesser of: · 80% of the purchase price (if a purchase) · 80% of the "as is" appraised value · Maximum loan amount minus cost to complete	**Bank REO or Distressed Sale** Limited to the lesser of: · 80% of the purchase price (if a purchase) · 80% of the "as is" appraised value · Maximum loan amount minus cost to complete **Non-Distressed Sale or Refinance** Limited to the lesser of: · 75% of the purchase price (if a purchase) · 75% of the "as is" appraised value · Maximum loan amount minus cost to complete	**Bank REO or Distressed Sale** Limited to the lesser of: · 70% of the purchase price (if a purchase) · 70% of the "as is" appraised value · Maximum loan amount minus cost to complete **Non-Distressed Sale or Refinance** Limited to the lesser of: · 65% of the purchase price (if a purchase) · 65% of the "as is" appraised value · Maximum loan amount minus cost to complete
New Construction & Building Lots (Construction or Development)			
Maximum LTV	Limited to the lesser of: · 75% of the total project cost · 70% of the "as complete" appraised value	Limited to the lesser of: · 70% of the total project cost · 65% of the "as complete" appraised value	Limited to the lesser of: · 65% of the total project cost · 60% of the "as complete" appraised value
Maximum Initial Advance (for construction loans)	Limited to the lesser of: · 75% of the lot purchase price (if a purchase) · 75% of the "as is" appraised value · Maximum loan amount minus cost to complete	Limited to the lesser of: · 70% of the purchase price (if a purchase) · 70% of the "as is" appraised value · Maximum loan amount minus cost to complete	Limited to the lesser of: · 65% of the purchase price (if a purchase) · 65% of the "as is" appraised value · Maximum loan amount minus cost to complete
All Transactions			
Maximum Loan Amount	$1,000,000	Lesser of 750,000 per unit or $5,000,000	$3,000,000
Minimum Property Values	$125,000	$75,000 per unit	Greater of $75,000 per unit or $200,000
Property DSCR	Not calculated	Pro forma of 1.25 or greater, if property is intended to be income-producing.	Pro forma of 1.25 or greater
Other	Must be non-owner occupied	Must be non-owner occupied. New construction projects must be fully permitted.	Must generally be eight units or fewer.

Contact us at: www.renovationconstructionloan.com or 407-476-2300

Program Overview	This program is designed to provide short-term financing for properties undergoing renovations, development, or stabilization. Each transaction must be accompanied by a documented property improvement or transition plan that will allow the loan to be paid off during the loan term (either through property sale or refinance into a permanent loan).
Loan Terms	Interest-only loan terms of six months to twenty-four months are available. Monthly interest payments will be required with the full principal due at maturity.
Eligible Borrowers	Borrowers must typically be business entities or corporations. Individual US citizens may be accepted on a case-by-case basis.
Eligible States	DC, FL, MD, NC, SC, VA
Ineligible Properties	Special purpose properties, environmentally impaired properties, properties with limited market acceptance, residential properties that will be used by the owners as primary residences or second homes.
Appraisal Requirements	An interior/exterior appraisal must be obtained for all collateral properties. Appraisals of commercial and development projects must be performed by an appraiser holding the MAI designation.
Site Inspections	An onsite review of all collateral properties must be performed by a LYNK representative prior to closing.
Cross Collateralization	Cross collateralization with additional properties will be considered provided that LYNK obtains a valid lien on the additional collateral.
Personal Guarantee	Personal guarantees are typically required from all property owners.
Environmental Report	A Phase I Environmental Site Inspection will be required if the subject property (or the surrounding neighborhood) exhibits potentially hazardous features or is of a type that may reasonably be subject to environmental impairment.
Prepayment Penalties	Prepayment penalties are generally not required, but may be utilized in certain deal structures.

Obtain loan servicing and accounting software – There are a ton of loan servicing systems in the marketplace and depending on your budget and the number of loans you plan to manage at any one time, you should chose the most appropriate one. Most loan servicing systems have accounting modules or reporting built into them. My companies have utilized many different servicing systems over the years and we have mostly utilized QuickBooks for our internal accounting. Obviously a larger company can purchase accounting software that best suit their needs.

Loan closing documents – The documents you want to use vary depending on what type of loans you want to make. As a private lender, I only do commercial loans so my loan documents are all geared toward these type of loans. Once you have identified an attorney to handle your closing, that attorney should have a set of documents for you to use and likely these documents can be modified toward your lending strategy. I would suggest the following list of documents to be included in your loan files but certain states have state specific requirements that are not included in the list here:

1. Loan note
2. Deed of trust or mortgage
3. Commercial loan affidavit
4. Loan agreement
5. Personal guarantee
6. Title certification
7. Adverse change agreement
8. Compliance agreement
9. Agreement to cooperate

Title company requirements – One of the most important aspects of risk management when lending money secured by real estate is to make sure you have a lenders title insurance policy. This insures the lender should a title issue or defect show up once the loan has closed. It is very important that the lender obtain a first lien letter (assuming the lender is in first lien position) and gap coverage. The title company will know what a "first lien letter" is and how to provide you "gap" coverage. Gap coverage basically insures that you as the lender are insured in the first lien position and covers the period of time the title abstractor performed the abstract to when the loan was closed.

If you are using a title company to close your loan, make sure that either your title company as an attorney or your attorney is clear that you as private lender are requiring that all insurance coverages be in place to provide first lien coverage.

To make it easier for the reader I will list out the title insurance suggested documentation below:

1. Obtain title commitment or binder prior to loan closing naming who the new lender will be and stating the new lender will be in 1st lien position
2. Obtain gap coverage and an insured closing protection letter from the title company
3. Have a meeting with the title company to inform them about obtaining evidence of the borrower from 2 forms of ID at closing
4. Once the loan is closed, make sure you follow up within 60 days of closing to obtain evidence your mortgage or deed of trust was recorded in the county courthouse.

OK, so now you know what the benefits and requirements of becoming your own private lender and doing it on your own are, so let's examine them and what should you review when deciding to invest in a loan pool or mortgage fund. Before we answer the question let's make sure you as the reader and possible investor are clear on what I mean in saying "mortgage loan pool" or "mortgage loan fund."

What is a Mortgage Pool?

A *mortgage pool* is a group of loans that are likely of similar types, where you as the investor own a small percentage of each of the loans. You could own a large or small percentage of the pool or a large or small percentage of each loan depending on your investment amount and the size and structure of the pool. The most typical way an investor invests or has an ownership in the mortgage loan pool is through a loan participant or loan participation agreement. With the loan participation agreement, each investor's name is possibly on the mortgage or it could be an assignment of participation by the originating lender. Let's look at an example of what I am talking about below:

o   The loan is closing in the name of ABC lender
o   10 loans are in the pool
o   The total loan amounts are $2,000,000
o   A total of 7 investors own the loan pool
o   Each investor has a different amount invested totaling the 2 million
o   For this example, if you were the investor and put up $200,000, you would own 10% of the pool
o   So in this example, you would be given a loan participation agreement from ABC lender that assigns you a 10% participant owner in the total of the 10 mortgages. You could record the assignment in the courthouse.

What is a Mortgage Fund?

A mortgage fund is fundamentally the same as a mortgage pool, but it is likely to be structured as a company that owns the mortgages whereby you own shares or membership interest in the company. The company owns the mortgages as its primary assets. Unlike a pool, you are not assigned an ownership in each loan, rather a proportional ownership in the company that owns the loans.

OK, please tell me the differences to an investor investing in a pool vs. a fund?

From my perspective, there is very little risk difference to capital loss in a pool vs a fund if the investment is set the same from a percentage standpoint. If you own 10% of a loan pool of 10 loans or 10% of the company that owns the 10 loans it is virtually the same. The main difference can be when investing in a loan pool you likely have investment money tied specifically to a specific loan. In the example above you have $200,000 tied up in 10 loans or $20,000 per loan and one of the loans goes into default, so your investment in that one loan is subject to the results of what would happen in a collection action and the resulting outcome of the sale of that one asset. In other words, when you have a specific allocation of ownership in specific loans, typically each investor is subject to the events of each loan vs. the events of the entire pool. Not all pools work this way but this is the way it worked when investors invested in my loan pools over the years.

Investing in a Mortgage Fund

Investing in a mortgage fund should be the same as investing in any business. The questions to ask are likely the same basic questions in dealing with risk, but let's examine the list of questions and answers I have outlined for you as investor. Keep in mind that each mortgage pool or fund is different and the questions could vary based on the fund strategy. When assessing the risk of the specific mortgage fund there are too many areas that could cause the fund to perform poorly, however the basics of the "risk profile" of the fund can be uncovered by a long due diligence process. Let's start with the suggested questions to ask below:

1. *How long has the fund been in existence?*
2. *How has the fund performed since inception?*
3. *How many assets has the fund loaned on?*
4. *How many assets went into default?*
5. *How long has the fund manager been managing mortgage assets?*
6. *Did the fund manager manage a previous mortgage fund?*
7. *Does the fund manager have any documented previous experience?*
8. *How many employees are in the fund?*
9. *What is the level of experience of the employees?*

10. *What geographic footprint does the fund lend?*
11. *What are minimum and maximum loan sizes the fund can loan?*
12. *What are the management fees?*
13. *Does the manager have any of their own money invested in the fund?*
14. *How does the manager get paid?*
15. *If the fund performs poorly how does it affect the manager?*
16. *What type of loans does the fund make?*
17. *Does the fund have any concentration in one type of mortgage or asset?*
18. *Does the fund have a loan to one borrower limit?*
19. *What are the projected default rates?*
20. *Does the fund have loan loss reserves or assumes the loss at time of actual loss occurrence?*
21. *What on-line access do I have as investor to the fund assets?*
22. *What level of transparency do I have to the funds loan servicing?*
23. *What level of access do I have to the loan documentation?*
24. *How long is my investment locked up?*
25. *What is the income waterfall?*
26. *Are there monthly or quarterly distributions if any distributions at all?*
27. *Do I have access to the monthly financials?*
28. *Does the fund obtain annual audits?*
29. *Can I obtain investor references that have invested in mortgages with the fund manager?*
30. *Who is the largest investor in the fund?*
31. *What due diligence has previously been performed on the fund and is this information available?*
32. *Does the fund use leverage or has debt on the books?*
33. *If the fund uses debt to increase the fund, what is the cost of the debt?*
34. *If debt is used, what is the interest spread between borrowers' note rates and the debt?*
35. *What are the basic covenants of the debt holders?*
36. *Was a site visit to the fund office performed?*
37. *Does the fund accept retirement funds?*
38. *Does the fund accept ERISA money?*
39. *Is the fund subject to UBTI?*

Chapter Summary

- ❖ If you as the investor only want an investment and not to actively work a business, you should invest in a mortgage fund and not do it on your own.
- ❖ If you want to work actively on your investment, consider being your own private lender.
- ❖ If you do it on your own as a private lender make sure you have proper loan documents created.
- ❖ If you do it on your own, go see every property and speak with every borrower directly yourself.
- ❖ If you only have $500,000 or less to invest, I would suggest investing in a mortgage fund rather than doing it on your own.
- ❖ Don't do it on your own unless you have your mastermind group lined up.
- ❖ If you invest in a fund, make sure you have obtained answers to the due diligence list.
- ❖ Don't put all your money with one fund.
- ❖ Personally interview the fund manager at his or her office.
- ❖ Personally interview at least 5 references of past investors of the fund manager.
- ❖ Take the position that I take, don't trust words only, try to document what you can as fact.

Be The Bank:

Chapter 9:
Getting Started as a Private Lender

HERE'S WHAT WE COVER IN THIS CHAPTER

- **Organizing your private lending business**
- **Determining loan pricing**
- **Marketing for the business**
- **Servicing the loans**

Now you have decided to do it on your own and start your own business as a private mortgage lender or perhaps you simply want to directly manage your own mortgage loan investments and not entrust someone else with your money. I support this thinking otherwise I would not have written this book.

I would like to go back to briefly explain again why we want to become **The Bank** and to be the lender to others. I get excited when I can explain to people about lending money, because everyone knows that banks lend money but so few individuals ever think about themselves becoming the bank. Just in case, let me list my reasons for you.

1. You get to secure your investments with real estate.
2. You get a defined income or interest return provided the borrower pays you each month.
3. You get to manage your own investment or retirement money versus someone else.
4. The returns can be considerably higher than MOST other investments.

5. You can build your own part time or full time business.
6. You can have fun doing one of the oldest businesses.

OK, now that I have you re-energized and given you the reasons to continue reading this very boring book you will want to officially get started.

In chapter 8 we took a deeper dive into being a private lender and in this chapter we will organize the steps you need to take and explain somewhat on what we covered in that last chapter.

LET'S BEGIN BY ORGANIZING AND SETTING UP THE BUSINESS

Step # 1 – *Determine if you need a state license to provide mortgage loans* – Each state is different about license requirements if you are lending your own money. Most of the states do not require a license to do commercial loans only as a private lender. My advice is to speak with your real estate attorney and have him or her provide the legal opinion on state licensing.

Step #2 – *Create your lending criteria*. Depending on how much money you have to invest and if you are planning to open a private lending business or just make a few investments, your actions will vary. If you are just wanting to make a few loans a year with your money, then you do not need a set of guidelines or loan programs. If you have a sizable sum of money to invest in a private mortgage business, you should create loan parameters. In chapter 8, I provided the guidelines from the LYNK Capital Mortgage fund for your review. I do not want to repeat everything in chapter 8 and chapters 2 & 4, but I did want to suggest specific lending parameters again for you as you begin in your new investment strategy or in your new private lending business.

SUGGESTED LENDING PARAMETERS

- o **Location of real estate collateral – within 3 hours of where you live**
- o **Loan type – Closed end fixed rate commercial mortgages**
- o **Loan position – First liens only**
- o **Property types – Commercial or residential investment property only**

o   **Maximum loan-to-value -70%, target 65% or less**
o   **Loan term – Maximum due in 3 years, either interest only or 30 year amortization**

Once of you have established the mortgage loan product parameters, next is to review the loan documentation.

Step # 3 – *Setup your team or what I call the mastermind group.* – In chapter 8 we listed letters a-g below. Let's provide a little more details on this list.

a. *Locate a closing & real estate attorney* experienced with private lenders – If you already know of a real estate attorney or a loan closing title attorney then this is the person I am referring to. You want a legal representative when acting as a lender to guide you on licensing laws, lending laws, loan closing documents, and title related issues. You should interview several attorneys based on experience, representing private lenders and the location and type of mortgages you want to make. Sometimes the legal expert is not the real estate expert and often not the title expert so it is import to try to locate an attorney that knows the lending laws, real estate laws, and can prepare loan documents in the location you are lending. It is very easy to obtain title insurance from someone other than the lawyer or law firm.

b. *Locate a dwelling insurance company* in case you or the borrower needs fire, liability, flood, and other types of property insurance. This needs to be a requirement for all loans that sufficient fire and liability coverage is in place and where you or your company is named as loss payee. Sometimes the borrowers do not pay the insurance later in the loan life and you are forced to place a fire and liability policy in place. This is called "forced place insurance" and very few insurance companies will write this insurance but you will need it eventually but not likely at the start of your lending.

c. *Locate a title insurance company* – All lenders need to protect themselves against title defects and need assurance that their lien on the property is perfected. The protection of this comes from a title insurance policy. I expanded on this in chapter 8 about obtaining gap coverage, insured closing protection letter, and also obtain the title companies' general business liability policy. The key is to make sure that even though there is the slightest chance that the title abstractor or the title company made a mistake, there are several ways to protect your investment. Do not ever close a loan without title insurance.

d. *Locate appraisers in your defined market* – Even though I have 31 years of making loans and even though I drive out to see every asset we loan money on, I still want an independent third party report on the property. You might find this interesting but one of the main reasons to obtain an appraisal by a third party is that the mortgage you originate could actually be sold in the future in the event you want to liquidate or just exit the lending business and if your loan files are complete and include a proper third party evaluation of the collateral it will allow you to more easily convert your loan into cash. When I first became a private lender with my money and friends and family's money, I did not require appraisals and a few years later I wanted to liquidate about 5 million of loans and could not without appraisals. The appraiser list does not have to be long, but should include experienced individuals, who live or work within 1 hour or less of the subject property that the appraiser is evaluating. Get a price list and a copy of their license and insurance. In my career, I have had an appraiser really let me down and I had to file a suit against him and his insurance carrier.

e. *Locate realtors or auctioneers* – I often will get an opinion of an experienced realtor in addition to the appraisal and my own site inspection. Perhaps this is overkill but realtors often have a more realistic view of the properties' location and marketability. It also allows me to line up the potential listing agent should I have to foreclose.

f. *Locate an environmental company* - In case you decide to lend on industrial or manufacturing properties, you will need to have an environmental company lined up to perform phase 1 and 2 reports. Most of us do not do a lot of environmentally sensitive loans however should you want to lend on this type of property, you will want to require environmental reports that state your collateral is free of environmental issues.

g. **_Locate licensed contractors_** - In the event you decide to lend to borrowers that want to use the loan funds to fix up or construct the real estate, you should have a knowledgeable contractor that can perform an inspection prior to closing and during the loan advance. I also like to have a contractor handy in the event I foreclose on the property and need to fix it up.

h. **_Locate a foreclosure or collection attorney_** – Prior to closing any loans, you should know the real estate foreclosure laws so that your loan documents are consistent with the collection laws of the state and that you are fully prepared to take legal action should a borrower default.

<u>Step # 4</u> - **_Create and finalize the loan decision and file document requirements_** – This is where you organize the process and procedures of the loan decision into a manual. As I mentioned previously in this chapter, if you are only going to lend on a handful of loans a year it makes little sense to develop a loan matrix, loan guidelines, lending policies and procedures. My hope is the readers of this book, who are excited about what they are learning, will invest their money with a professional mortgage expert or will want to begin a new business, either part time or full time as a private lender so the creation of lending policies and procedures makes sense. In chapter 8, I include the table of contents for the LYNK Capital Mortgage Fund so we do not need to repeat it here, but I would like to point out the policies and procedures just to guide you on what information you want in each loan file and how you want to make your loan decisions. For example, what if you forget to get a fire insurance policy on a property and the day after you lend someone $200,000, the property burns to the ground? You call your borrower and let him know he still has to repay you and he says: "What, I just lost my house, I have no way of paying you back $200,000 because the dirt is only worth $50,000." I can keep going with reasons to have a set of guidelines, if nothing more than to keep you organized and the files properly documented.

Your lending guidelines should include underwriting, processing, and closing requirements, loan file documentation, and loan servicing policy.

Lending guidelines and internal policies can be written to suit your specific goals as private lender. One of the areas you should organize before you get started is the loan file checklist and required items you want in the loan files. This way you have an organized way to check what you need or want to have.

Loan file suggested list:

1. Borrower application – I have included it in the appendix
2. Borrower credit authorization – I have included it in the appendix
3. Borrower financials, such as tax returns, financial statements, asset accounts
4. Property information to include the appraisal, comps, site inspection, realtor opinion, etc.
5. Insurance and title information – Fire, liability & title insurance
6. Closing documents – All loan closing documents
7. Post-closing items – Checklists & recorded documents
8. Miscellaneous – Everything else

<u>Step # 5</u> - *Set up your software systems as desired* –The volume of loans and the total amount of money you have to invest will drive the decisions on the software required to operate properly your private lending business. Most mortgage companies include the list below in their information technology strategy and solution:

1. A website
2. Loan origination and processing software
3. Loan servicing software

The list I have included in this step can vary greatly from investor to investor. You need NONE of it, but you should have ALL of it in your business. A private investor or lender who plans to lend on a handful of loans a year needs none of the list. For those readers that want to build a private lending business I recommend considering each of these I.T. actions. Let's take a look at each one.

<u>Website suggestions</u>

The website should include all information about the lending programs and lending areas. It should include how to submit the loan, contact information, and a basic overview of company.

Loan Origination, loan processing, and loan servicing software

There are many companies providing loan origination, loan processing, and loan servicing software. My suggestion is that you search on-line for what you want. It is difficult to direct you as companies and software change all the time.

Step #6 - *Setting loan pricing* - Each investor can set his is or her own loan pricing levels. What I have learned is that the location of the property, the loan amount, the property type, and the borrower's profile all play a role in what the borrower is willing to pay for the use of the money. I travel the country doing investor seminars and discuss what interest rates borrowers pay to get private mortgage funds. In California, it appears very difficult to charge a borrower 13% for a first mortgage, whereas in Maryland most private lenders I know charge 12-15% interest to ALL the borrowers. The loan pricing guideline that I suggested in previous chapters should probably be 4-10% over the 10-year treasury. I state this because the argument is about a "risk adjusted return." You might be saying to yourself: "Hey, I thought the risks were minimal if you properly lend the money? So why there is such a high interest rate?" Most likely, the borrower has already tried to obtain money from a bank or has concluded that he or she cannot borrow the money from a bank. Borrowers may not know better, but in most cases borrowers look for the best rates they can find and at some point recognize that they need to borrow money to complete the real estate purchase or make money with the real estate. Keep in mind that we are NOT referring to consumer lending as this book and the direction to our readers is to make ONLY commercial or business needs loans secured by real estate.

Step # 7 - *Getting the loans* - Many people who know I am writing this book have asked why would I give away for almost free the "secret sauce." Not sure it is a secret but more of a strategy that has worked for me over the past 30 years as a private lender. My suggestion is to market for loans in the areas you want to lend with a specific target on the type of loans. Consider some of the marketing options listed below:

- Generate a marketing flyer that outlines your lending products.
- Get your website up and running so that it explains the loan types and how to submit a loan.

- Obtain a list of all the mortgage brokers, realtors, title companies, accountants in the marketplace you want to target and call, email, mail, and/or visit to introduce yourself to them.
- Go to real estate investors' meetings.
- Go to real estate brokers' meetings.
- Meet with auctioneers and advise them of your product.

Once the marketplace knows you have capital to lend, the deals will begin to flow. I do not have statistics on this next statement but my estimate is that banks only provide 50%-65% of the mortgage capital to commercial mortgage borrowers. The data is very limited on the number of private lenders or the number of private mortgage loans made each year so my figures are purely guesswork. That suggests that a large percentage of borrowers need private funding. What I can likely say with confidence is that some borrowers will not qualify by the normal bank guidelines and will be forced to borrow from private sources of capital.

Step # 8 - *Servicing the loans* – So now you have provided the loans and you need to service the loan and protect your income stream. I will provide just a few ideas or opinions on servicing your loan.

a. If you have many loan outsource servicing. There are numerous loan servicing companies throughout the United States that are excellent at servicing loans. Many of these companies service tens of thousands of loans and have excellent technology and tools to do a much better job than you can.

b. Do not be very flexible when it comes to collections or legal action upon loan defaults. I have rarely experienced a "business borrower" not take all the rope you give them so do not give them any rope. I apparently had a reputation for being a jerk and it was mainly because my belief that when a person borrows money from you, they need to repay it or turn the property over and walk away. I just do not take kindly to that, because when they need the money you are a saint and they use your money to make money for themselves and then when you have to collect the money, all of a sudden, they hate you and you are a bad guy.

c. If you are servicing the loans yourself, NEVER give out your home address or home phone number on anything. Setup a PO Box number for mortgage payments. I would not even provide a physical office address because you never know what could happen with a nasty borrower.

d. If you are servicing the loans yourself, do NOT say the money is yours even if it is. You can say some of the money or you are part of a group that is lending the money but you do not want your borrowers to rely solely on you for decisions. I always used "loan committee" or "my partners" when discussing decisions before and after closing the loan. It is always best if the borrower thinks they are borrowing from a "company" rather than a "person."

Chapter Summary

❖ Managing your own capital as a private investor can be wonderfully rewarding financially and professionally versus having someone else manage your money.

❖ Before you begin building your own private lending business, organize the business.

❖ Make sure you have your mastermind group established before you begin.

❖ Follow my 8-step process to organizing the business of private lending.

❖ Make sure you have the loan file documentation worked out before you begin.

❖ Getting the loans is easy.

❖ Do not provide borrowers your home address or telephone number.

BE THE BANK:

Chapter 10:
Why You Want to "BE THE BANK":
A Look at the Financial Model of Private Lending

HERE'S WHAT WE COVER IN THIS CHAPTER

- **Why I love BEING THE BANK**
- **The private lending financial model**
- **The use of debt in leveraging capital and returns**
- **Book Summary**

I titled this book "Be the Bank" because I have enjoyed 30 years of being the bank in some form or another. It was a very interesting and fun career. This is the last chapter in this book and I am hoping that you have learned a lot and benefited from its information as an investor looking for investment alternatives or becoming your own private mortgage lender. For me, this business has represented financial freedom and doing something that has a great benefit to others. You can drop me in any city in this country and I can make a high six-figure income within the first year because of my knowledge in lending others money. It is not just about my success but it is actually more about the number of people that I know will benefit from using private money. The key to success in lending is knowing exactly what to do and how to do it. Throughout this book, I mentioned two questions for you to ponder.

Question 1 – "If it's so easy, why doesn't everyone do it"

Question 2 – "If you have a formula that makes you money, why would you tell it to everyone who reads this book and create competition?"

Consider my comments below:

o *I know the formula for success as a private lender and I know it took years to learn.*

o *Almost EVERYONE who is over 21 years benefits from borrowing money so the product is widely used by most adults, as most adults borrow money at some point in their life.*

o *It does take months or years to learn how to lend money safely.*

o *People typically would rather use your money than theirs to make more money.*

o *Money is simply a commodity.*

o *Most people turn to banks when they need to borrow money.*

o *Banks cannot take much risk.*

o *There are plenty of people who need to borrow money from me but there are as many people who would pay me to teach them.*

My major point to make to the readers is that almost *every bank and credit union makes the majority of its money lending it out but the* **mainstream population** *does not invest at all, including part of their retirement or investment funds in the same business that almost every bank in the world invests. Just think about that for a minute. It is an investment that makes sense for a bank but not for most of the population? Well, let me tell you that it certainly is.*

The Lending Model
The summary of what your investment in a mortgage should look like:

Loan money to a business related borrower secured by a 1st mortgage on real estate for a period of 3 years or less whereby your loan does not exceed 65-70% of the value of the underlying collateral. The interest rate should be at least 3-5% over the 10-year treasury rates and can be interest only payments due monthly.

For example, you as the investor have $100,000 to invest. You decide to lend it out secured by a first mortgage on a property valued at $160,000. The loan agreement states that you are charging 10% interest each year and collecting interest only payments of $833.33 each month. The borrower needs the money for 2-3 years until he or she improves their credit and can refinance the loan with the local banks. The property is rented for $1200 a month. Assuming the borrower paid you each month, what is your annual return on invested capital? It is 10% of course or $10,000 of income on the $100,000 you invested.

Annual returns of 10% are not bad, and actually most would say that there are quite good. Consider the use of leverage or debt in this scenario. Let's say you only had $50,000 but the borrower needed $100,000 to make the deal work. Perhaps you could borrow the other $50,000 from a home equity line or from a line against a stock portfolio? Assuming you could borrow the additional $50,000 at 5% from your local bank, let's look at 3 examples beginning with a no leverage loan, a 1:1 leverage loan and a 3:1 leverage scenario.

Mortgage investment example # 1 – No leverage

You invest $100,000 in a loan to borrower at 10% annually or $10,000 per year in interest income

Return on investment example # 1: You loan $100,000 at 10% and earn $10,000 income and 10% annual return.

Mortgage investment example # 2 – 1:1 leverage

You provide a $100,000 loan to the borrower: $50,000 was from you, and you borrowed the other $50,000 from a bank to lend the total of $100,000.

The $50,000 was borrowed from the bank and was secured by several options: the $100,000 mortgage, your stocks, or a home equity line on another property you own. The payment on the $50,000 at 5% interest is $2,500 annually so the math looks like:

$10,000 in interest income collected from the borrower annually.
$2,500 in interest expense on the $50,000 borrowed at 5% per year.
$7,500 net income collected on the loan transaction each year.

Return on investment example # 2: You loaned $100,000 to the borrower, and only used $50,000 of own money and $50,000 borrowed from the bank. You earn $7500 in net income or $15% annually on the $50,000 initial Capital.

Mortgage investment example # 3 – 3:1 leverage

Consider a scenario where you loaned out $100,000 to a borrower, but borrowed $75,000 from a bank and only invested $25,000 of your own capital.

$10,000 in annual interest revenue collected from the borrower.
$3,750 in annual interest expense on the borrowed $75,000 at 5%.
$6,250 in net income annually.

Return on investment example # 3: You loaned $100,000 to borrower, and you only used $25,000 of own money and $75,000 borrowed from a bank. You will earn $6,250 in net income or 25% annually on the $25,000 of your own capital.

Summary of the 3 examples:

Gross loan to borrower	Private investors' capital (Equity)	Private investors' leverage (Debt at 5% annually)	Leverage ratio	Net return on Equity
$100,000	$100,000	$0	0	10% annually
$100,000	$50,000	$50,000	1:1	15% annually
$100,000	$25,000	$75,000	3:1	25% annually

I am sure many of you who are experienced bankers and investors are saying to yourself: "Yeah, but you had to borrow the $75,000 and that is using debt and leveraging therefore increasing the risk to the capital." The concept of taking on debt to increase return can be good or bad depending on what happens to the overall recovery of the total loan in the event of a foreclosure. I would argue that the "risk adjusted" returns can be completely in balance if the loan collateral and loan underwriting is done properly. I point your attention to a white paper that my colleague Matt Brothers and I wrote on the use of leverage in our private mortgage lending Fund we run.

To Leverage or Not to Leverage?
By Ben Lyons & Matt Brothers

> *lev·er·age*: 1. the ratio of a company's loan capital (debt) to the value of its common stock (equity). 2. the use of credit or borrowed capital to increase the earning potential of stock. 3. use borrowed capital for (an investment), expecting the profits made to be greater than the interest payable.

While raising capital for LYNK Capital Real Estate Fund 1 (the Fund), we have been asked many times about leverage. Many of these questions stem from a lack of knowledge about, or practical experience with, leveraged funds. Certainly, there have been many cases in recent years of organizations and financial institutions that were leveraged well beyond their means; however, the purpose of the following information is to provide clarity to potential investors on LYNK Capital's approach to leverage and risk management.

This whitepaper will outline the strategy that LYNK Capital plans to use to leverage the Fund, the projected financial impact to the Fund, and the positive and negative risks of leveraging. Please note that the views or opinions expressed herein are the opinion of Ben Lyons, Managing Director and Matt Brothers, VP of the LYNK Capital Fund. Additionally, this document assumes the reader already has a basic understanding of LYNK Capital's fund offerings.

Fund Overview

LYNK Capital's business plan for Fund 1 can be summarized as:

- Loans will be made to owners of transitional real estate projects for terms of between six months and two years.
- Loans will be first mortgages with an average portfolio LTV of 60% or less.
- Leverage will be employed at a 3:1 ratio to increase investor returns.

Benefits of Leverage

The primary benefit of leverage is to increase the returns earned by Fund investors. By leveraging the Fund's equity to acquire outside debt, the Fund can increase the size of its loan portfolio and earn additional income from the spread between the portfolio interest rate and the cost of the debt.

To illustrate this benefit, the following table shows a simplified pro-forma of four scenarios, ranging from no leverage up to a leverage ratio of 3:1. All scenarios assume loan income of 13% and a cost of debt of 6.0%:

Leverage Scenario	No debt	1:1	2:1	3:1
Equity	$25,000,000	$25,000,000	$25,000,000	$25,000,000
Debt	$0	$25,000,000	$50,000,000	$75,000,000
Total Loans:	$25,000,000	$50,000,000	$75,000,000	$100,000,000
Interest Income (13%)	$3,250,000	$6,500,000	$9,750,000	$13,000,000
Debt Payments (6%)	$0	$1,500,000	$3,000,000	$4,500,000
Provision for loan loss*	$300,000	$600,000	$900,000	$1,200,000
Net Income	$2,950,000	$4,400,000	$5,850,000	$7,300,000
ROE	12%	18%	23%	29%

From this, the benefit of leverage can be clearly seen; by increasing the leverage ratio to 3:1, the gross fund return is increased by 17% over the base (no debt) scenario.

*Provision for loan loss in this model is calculated using an 8% default rate and an average 15% principal loss on those defaulted loans. It should be noted that, assuming a 60% original LTV, a 15% principal loss would require a nearly 49% drop in the value of the underlying collateral.

Risks of Leverage

In the wake of the financial meltdown of 2007-2010, many investors are leery of leveraged investment funds. Indeed, during this time period, property values declined precipitously, default rates spiked, and many highly levered Wall Street funds (often structured as collateralized debt obligations or CDOs) collapsed with near-total equity losses. At question is the role that leverage played in the collapse of those CDOs – was leverage the primary cause or was something else at play?

Upon examination of those CDOs, it can be seen that, in addition to employing leverage, they were also backed by risky loans with low levels of excess collateral available to absorb market shocks. So how did that lack of collateral impact performance? And will LYNK Capital's more conservative collateral requirements perform better?

Effects of Portfolio LTV

Losses to equity owners occur when loans default and the current value of the underlying collateral is less than the outstanding loan balance (plus legal costs to foreclose). For this reason, the value of the underlying collateral (measured by the portfolio's Loan-to-Value ratio (LTV)) is of great importance when evaluating the overall risk of any investment, whether leveraged or not.

To begin evaluating the risk of LYNK Capital's Fund relative to those 2007-vintage CDOs, the LTV structure of each must be compared. According to data published in a Harvard research paper, the average combined LTV on asset-backed CDOs outstanding in the mid-2000s was 85.45%.[4] This compares to a forecasted average LTV of 60% or less in LYNK Capital's Fund 1.

[4]Green, Richard K. and Susan M. Wachter. "The American Mortgage in Historical and International Context." The Journal of Economic Perspectives, Vol. 19, No. 4. (Autumn, 2005), pp. 93-114

Based on this difference in LTV, how would each fund be expected to perform during an extreme market shock, such as the events of 2007-2009? During the period, two significant events occurred that caused many CDOs to fail:

- Nationwide property values declined by 32%.[5]
- Default rates on CDOs rapidly increased to 43% (from an average of 8%).[6]

Using these data points, the following model can be constructed to show the projected equity losses in both a Wall Street CDO with an 85% LTV and the LYNK Capital Fund with a 60% LTV. For simplicity, both scenarios are constructed with no debt, and the only difference between the two is the average LTV of the portfolio:

	LYNK Capital	**Wall Street CDO**
A. Leverage:	None	None
B. LTV:	60%	85%
C. Equity:	$25,000,000	$25,000,000
D. Debt:	$0	$0
E. Loans (C+D):	$25,000,000	$25,000,000
F. Drop in Property Value	32%	32%
G. Legal Costs	8%	8%
H. Loss per Loan (B+F+G-100%):	0%	25%
I. Default Rate:	43%	43%
J. Equity Loss (H*I*E):	$0	$2,735,875
K. Equity Loss (%):	0%	11%

---

[5] http://www.hks.harvard.edu/m-rcbg/students/dunlop/2009-CDOmeltdown.pdf

[6] http://us.spindices.com/indices/real-estate/sp-case-shiller-us-national-home-price-index

From this, it can be seen that, based solely on the difference in LTV, the Wall Street CDO incurred an equity loss of 11% from the shock, while the proposed LYNK Capital Fund's equity was unaffected. This is attributable to the simple fact that LYNK Capital's conservative underwriting structure requires more collateral to be available to offset decreases in property value – the lower LTV of LYNK Capital's Fund allows it to absorb more than two and a half times the amount of property value decrease before incurring equity losses.

Addition of Leverage

The example above was constructed without any leverage - so what happens when debt is added? The following model uses the same assumptions as above, but adds leverage at a 3:1 ratio:

	LYNK Capital	**Wall Street CDO**
A. Leverage:	3:1	3:1
B. LTV:	60%	85%
C. Equity:	$25,000,000	$25,000,000
D. Debt:	$75,000,000	$75,000,000
E. Loans (C+D):	$100,000,000	$100,000,000
F. Drop in Property Value	32%	32%
G. Legal Costs	8%	8%
H. Loss per Loan (B+F+G-100%):	0%	25%
I. Default Rate:	43%	43%
J. Equity Loss (H*I*E):	$0	$10,943,500
K. Equity Loss (%):	0%	44%

The addition of the leverage to this model causes the losses of the Wall Street CDO to increase dramatically; however, the LYNK Capital fund remains unaffected. This is, again, due to the extra cushion of collateral provided by the lower LTV the LYNK Capital fund. From this, it can be seen that the amount of leverage has no effect on when equity losses occur (or how likely they are to occur), although leverage can increase losses that already exist.

The above model shows both funds using LYNK Capital's desired leverage ratio of 3:1, but is this a realistic comparison to those failed CDOs? It is somewhat difficult to state an average leverage ratio for mid-2000s CDOs due to disparate and complicated tranche structures, but for this comparison an average leverage ratio of 10:1 will be assumed (and there are many cases in which CDOs used much higher leverage ratios in certain tranches). So how does a 10:1 Wall Street CDO compare to LYNK Capital's proposed 3:1 fund?

	LYNK Capital	**Wall Street CDO**
A. Leverage:	3:1	10:1
B. LTV:	60%	85%
C. Equity:	$25,000,000	$25,000,000
D. Debt:	$75,000,000	$250,000,000
E. Loans (C+D):	$100,000,000	$275,000,000
F. Drop in Property Value	32%	32%
G. Legal Costs	8%	8%
H. Loss per Loan (B+F+G-100%):	0%	25%
I. Default Rate:	43%	43%
J. Equity Loss (H*I*E):	$0	$30,094,625
K. Equity Loss (%):	0%	120%

At a leverage ratio of 10:1, the Wall Street CDO would experience a total loss of equity from the shock while, again, the LYNK Capital 3:1 fund remains unaffected. This clearly demonstrates how LYNK Capital's Fund could remain solvent, even with leverage, during a market shock that could cause less conservative CDOs to fail.

Conclusions

From these models, LYNK Capital draws two broad conclusions:

- The LTV of the loan portfolio is a significant factor in determining whether losses are likely to occur. By constructing a portfolio with an average LTV of 60% or less, the Fund should be well-positioned to weather a substantial market shock, such as occurred during the period from 2007-2009.

- The use of leverage does not increase the likelihood that losses of equity will occur, (though leverage can amplify any losses that do occur). Due to the conservative LTV requirements of the Fund, LYNK Capital believes that the use of leverage represents a prudent and reasonable strategy for increasing investor returns.

In summary, LYNK Capital believes that, by employing conservative LTV requirements, its fund will be structured in a manner that is materially different from many of the leveraged Wall Street funds that have made headlines in recent years. Indeed, the models above demonstrate how LYNK Capital's proposed fund survives a shock equivalent to the events of 2007-2009 without significant loss, even with leverage being employed. LYNK Capital believes that combining conservative LTV requirements with the use of leverage in its fund (up to a 3:1 leverage ratio) represents a prudent and reasonable strategy for increasing investor returns while protecting its equity capital across a range of market shocks.

Disclaimers

Sections of this document contain forward-looking statements that reflect management's best judgment based on several factors that involve significant risks and uncertainties. Actual results could differ materially from those anticipated in these forward-looking statements as a result of a number of factors, including but not limited to risks such as future changes in property values and delinquency rates, the actual average LTV of the fund portfolio based on loans to be made in the future, and general economic conditions. Forward-looking information provided pursuant to the safe harbor established by recent securities legislation should be evaluated in the context of these factors.

We can definitely argue about leverage, but I would stand firm in stating that an investor who wants NO risk can just invest in Treasuries and not worry about risk to invested capital. The investor who wants to take a portion of his or her investment capital and leverage it to consistently earn 20% in annual returns completely secured by real estate can safely and aggressively build a nest egg for retirement.

A MESSAGE FROM BEN TO YOU AS A HOPEFULLY INSPIRED PRIVATE MORTGAGE INVESTOR.

I wanted to say thank you for reading my book and I look forward to your feedback. More importantly I look forward to knowing that I may have helped you, as an investor, to improve your investment strategy or have directed you in a new career as a private mortgage lender. If nothing else, I hope I provided an education on private mortgage lending and investing. My philosophy about our life here on Earth, which is very short, is that we need to positively impact others in good ways and help others to achieve their best as often as possible. It is not about the money we make or the things we have as the true measure of success. It is the people we have inspired and assisted along the way and after we are gone. I got very lucky at a young age of 18 when I skipped college and learned how to lend money on real estate. I would have liked to attend college, but I was having too much fun digging into my future at a young age and I was consumed with this specialized knowledge path very quickly. My ability to become self-sufficient by age 19 and to have acquired financial freedom by age 30 did more for my self-esteem than anything else I could imagine. This then propelled me to commit to helping to grow others wherever possible. Being the bank is NOT out of reach, regardless of your educational background or financial status. If you do not have any money, you can do what I did, take partners who had money and use their money to excel as "the bank."

I volunteer to teach two days a month at a wonderful school in Baltimore City called the Community School. The class is about personal finance and in that class I teach a lesson on leverage. My lesson teaches about how the truly successful learn to leverage many things: from people, ideas, money, and our time. I hope that many investors of all ages and net worth, learn to leverage this book and go out and become **the bank**. Let's not leave the lending of money to ONLY the regulated institutions we call a bank, because you too can "BE THE BANK."

Book Summary

- ❖ Becoming "the bank" is not easy, but it is not that hard to do once you learn how.
- ❖ Most adults, at some point in their lives, borrow money secured by real estate and that provides for a never ending supply of loans.
- ❖ Follow my lending model all the way to the bank to achieve 20% annual returns.
- ❖ Leverage, if used properly as a mortgage lender, can produce incredibly high rates of returns.
- ❖ The risk of utilizing leverage is minimized if the Loan-to-Values are below 60%.
- ❖ Finally, YOU CAN BE THE BANK.